Embracing Quincy

Our Journey Together

by

Katie Marsh

Copyright © 2013 Katie Marsh

First Paperbound Printing

Printed in the USA

All rights reserved. No part of this book may be reproduced in any form or transmitted by any means – electronic, mechanical, or otherwise – including photography, recording, or any information storage and retrieval system, without permission in writing from the author.

www.embracingquincy.com

Fifth Dimension Press

PO Box 531

Madawaska, ME 04756

Library of Congress Control Number: 2013934615

Cover design by Sherwin Soy

For

My Quincy Rose

Table of Contents

Chapter 1	The Kick	6
Chapter 2	Southern California to Northern Maine	9
Chapter 3	Our Family	19
Chapter 4	Honey, I Think the Kids are Psychic	27
Chapter 5	Shagging Dan	35
Chapter 6	Just Being	46
Chapter 7	Quincy	48
Chapter 8	Abortion	66
Chapter 9	Amnios and Ultrasounds	75
Chapter 10	Trisomy 18	81
Chapter 11	Proactive Sanity	85
Chapter 12	The Blessing Way	89
Chapter 13	Prayer in Numbers	94
Chapter 14	Buddha in the Storm	99
Chapter 15	Psychic Moments and Little G	118
Chapter 16	Other People's Miracles	126
Chapter 17	The Bias of the Blind	138
Chapter 18	A Fifth Dimension Being	142
Chapter 19	*Heroics* and Other Euphemisms	156
Chapter 20	Searching for Roots on a Farm	158
Chapter 21	Enter Willow, Stage Left	176
Chapter 22	Coincidences and Realities	184
Chapter 23	A Human Incubator	189
Chapter 24	Birthing Quincy	204
Chapter 25	The Futile Fight	209
Chapter 26	The Incredible and Inexplicable	221

Table of Contents

(continued)

Chapter 27	Healing	224
Chapter 28	Waiting for Mary Jo	231
Chapter 29	Big Changes and Unanswered Questions	238
Chapter 30	Yes	242
	About the Title	
	About the Author	
	Acknowledgments	
	Further Reading and Other Resources	
	The Most Important Section of This Book	

Chapter 1

The Kick

In silence we drove the five miles from the high-tech ultrasound office to Dan's parents' beach house to pick up the girls. We tried to act like everything was okay but it had been about five hours since we had dropped them off, so his parents looked worried.

"Everything okay?" his mom asked.

"No," I smiled, fighting back the tears. We gave her a brief version of what the doctor told us, then hurriedly packed up the truck with the girls and their many stuffed animals and sundries so we could make the hour-and-a-half trek back up the mountains to Julian before dark.

Thankfully, on the way home the girls fell asleep in the back of our pickup. It was a Ford F-250 that we bought a couple of weeks earlier so that we'd have enough room for three car seats in the roomy back seat yet still have enough utility to pick up hay for Dan's horse and make the rutted off-road journey through the mountain pass to reach our gold claim on the weekends.

"What do you think about this? Is he right?" I asked Dan.

"The equipment was pretty high tech. But it's an ultrasound; it's never foolproof. The amnio will tell us more," Dan tried to reassure me.

"Yeah, but it has its dangers. What if they poke her in the eye with the needle?" I paused for a while, still in major shock. I desperately felt like I wanted to run away from this problem but knew that I couldn't. Quincy and I were attached physically, emotionally and spiritually.

"What do you think about what the doctor said about 'some parents would terminate'?" I questioned Dan, testing the waters to gauge if we had the same thoughts about this subject. "I'm 22 weeks. I *feel* her moving inside of me."

At that exact moment I felt Quincy kick. And she kicked very hard—like never before. *And never afterwards.* She moved and kicked and thrashed around, so much so that I started to fret that she was in some kind of physical distress. Was the cord strangling her suddenly?

"Whoa," I exclaimed as I clutched my belly with both hands, startled and a bit frightened by the sudden violent movement. After a moment I sensed that she wasn't in physical danger. "Dan, feel this!" I whispered, trying not to wake up the kids. He removed his right hand from the steering wheel and allowed me to guide it to the correct spot on my belly.

Wide-eyed, I turned awkwardly in my seat to face Dan. "She *hears* me. She *knows* what I'm saying!"

Chapter 2

Southern California to Northern Maine

As I write, sitting at a coffee shop in Madawaska, a small town in Northern Maine, drinking a black coffee, I realize it hasn't even been a year since Quincy's birth. Although I'm excited to share our tumultuous story, it has been an extremely intense journey physically, emotionally, and spiritually. I find myself stalling because writing about it will be reliving the lowest parts of the journey along with its peaks.

There's snow on the ground outside with more falling intermittently all day as Christmas approaches. It's warmer on the days that it snows, as the cloud blanket above helps to insulate the earth. On sunny days in mid-winter it can be sinus-freezing cold with wind chill temperatures dipping to -40 F or lower. If you don't know what that sensation feels like, you've probably never lived someplace really cold—or your sinuses are extremely dry.

The light poles have been decorated with cords of lights that spiral up the posts ending with an old-fashioned bow and spray—very different from the flashy, evenly-spaced light blankets that cover the palm trees in San Diego this time of year.

Across the street is the house that we just purchased two and a half months ago. It's the first home I've ever been a part of purchasing. While I'm proud of this fact in the same way one feels who has just accomplished a major goal, I can't also help but feel the absurdity of it, too. Right now the bank really owns the house and we pay them until we don't have to any more. Then do we truly own it? Shouldn't shelter and land belong to all creatures, not just those lucky enough to afford it? Nevertheless, this is how we humans have structured our world so within that context I'm very grateful for our new home.

The house is a typical New England style residence built in 1930. Someone years ago divided it into three makeshift apartments. We live in the tiny back apartment next to the garage that houses my husband Dan's tire shop; two families inhabit the front apartments. The rents cover our mortgage and heating bill, allowing us to live very affordably, which is part of the reason we moved here from warm and sunny San Diego County.

People are very nice here, but you can tell they think we're crazy for relocating to Maine—they're just too polite to say so. Except for the United States border patrol agents a couple of blocks from where we live. We often drive across the bridge spanning the St. John River to Canada to shop or watch a movie. On the way back home one evening as we passed the check point, a border patrol agent said to us what everyone else in Madawaska is probably thinking, "San Diego to *Maine*! What are you guys running from?"

The big move to Madawaska took us 13 days. Thirteen days with our little girls, two bearded dragons, one blue heeler/border collie, one labradane and all of our stuff that we just "couldn't live without" in a Penske truck followed by me driving our 2001 Ford 4x4 pickup truck. As it turns out, we probably could have lived without 90 percent of what we dragged across country. But you never know this until you move or put your things in storage to travel for a while.

I always thought you could move anywhere in the US and feel pretty much at home. Of course it would be a little different because it's a new place with new faces. But Northern Maine is a whole kettle of lobster different than what I expected. Madawaska is a town of about 3,500 people. Most residents here are Acadian and speak French and English. In Edmundston, Canada, the small twin city across the St. John River, people speak French and maybe some English. The border is quite blurred here as you often find Canucks living here and Americans living in Edmundston with many families spread out on both sides of the border.

I learned some French in high school when it became my passion. We had a French exchange student stay with us for a short time, until my mother became jealous of her and made the girl return home prematurely. I briefly traveled to Europe on a 10-day high school trip, mostly to have the opportunity to check out Paris. Dan and the girls don't speak much French yet, but the girls are learning quickly in school.

Dan and I aren't ones to really do our homework when we decide to move somewhere. Economics is always the first motivator, followed closely by the thrill of adventure and novelty. And as most deliberate people probably suspect, impulsivity can bring unwanted surprises. Our first surprise in moving to Northern Maine was the five-block-long paper mill right next to our home. It is so close that if we sled down our hill, we would hit the side of the mill. Our very efficient and ebullient real estate agent failed to mention its existence to us. When we arrived here and asked about the proximity of the paper mill and its accompanying stench, her surprised response was, "Is that a problem for you?" That's what we get for buying a house sight unseen.

The second surprise in moving to Northern Maine has been the families. There are only a few last names here, and they're all French. When I say a few, I mean there's probably about 20 last names with four or five predominant family names that you see and hear every day. Moving here has felt like crashing someone's private party. Although almost everyone we have met has been very friendly and welcoming, I almost feel like we should have asked permission to move here first.

But I think our outsider status has boosted the morale of some of the residents. We hear over and over again people saying that they're glad young families are moving into the area instead of away to the bigger cities.

How did the Big Move come to be? It was the convergence of three situations that led to our move. We were renting a house in Julian, California, a small mountain community in the eastern part of San Diego County. Over the course of about three and a half years we became friends with the landlords and lived there peacefully, nurturing our little family and becoming a part of the community. One day our landlord friends decided they needed the shed on the property to store some supplies for the town's art guild. So they just took it over, ignoring our protestations. We value our privacy and we needed the storage space, too, we told them. After all, it was our shed, according to the lease.

Labor Day weekend, like in the beach areas, is one of the busiest weekends in Julian. We returned home from a trip for groceries "down the hill," as we called it, to find that someone from the art guild had let both of our dogs out of the yard in order to get into the shed. No one had called us first to ask if it would be okay to come over. Fortunately, our labradane, Koa, came bounding down our driveway when he saw our truck and shortly thereafter we received a call from a local restaurant asking us to retrieve our other dog, Buddy. We immediately gave our 30-day notice.

14

Difficulties can pile up simultaneously in life and it's not until later that we realize that they were really blessings cloaked in anguish. For years we had been trying to purchase property and build a farm. We would have done this for certain in Julian and settled down there to raise our family—if we could have afforded it.

"Dan, I don't care where it takes us, but I cannot rent one more day in my life," I said. "We're in our mid-40s and I've never owned a place and I hate renting. I want something to pass on to our kids one day so they never have to worry about having a place to call home."

"Let's do it," he said. "We'll find something we can afford on eBay."

But what about Dan's parents, I thought? They are in their mid-70s and the only family that lived close to us. We'd occasionally get together with Dan's sister, brothers, niece and the girls' cousins, but not as often because everyone is spread out all around Southern California. But Dan's mom and dad were the closest—about an hour and a half away in Encinitas, a beach community in San Diego County. The girls have gotten closer to them since we moved back to San Diego from Hawaii. Although they pretty much only saw their grandparents about once a month, I hated the idea of keeping them apart again.

But as fate would have it, on the same day we exchanged heated words with our landlords and gave notice, we learned that Dan's mom was moving back to her childhood hometown in Washington State.

So our home was gone and family was essentially gone. And we still had the burning desire to own something to pass down to the kids one day. We figured Dan's dad would go into hermit mode and not want to spend time with us unless we forced ourselves on him. So why live in one of the most expensive places in the country, incessantly struggling just to get by? Were we destined to forever rent a temporary home that wasn't ours, leaving ourselves vulnerable to the vagaries of impetuous landlords? What were we waiting for? So many people just talk of dreams that never come to fruition. Did we want to set that example for our kids, that dreams are just that and never something tangible?

If we were going to make a big move and live the life we both wanted, we should be willing to take a big risk. What we really wanted was to raise the girls on a farm and build an Earthship (http://www.earthship.org). Before we met, Dan and I both had the separate dreams of farm life—I just added the Earthship part. An Earthship is an off-grid home, meaning that it is not hooked up to any municipal water, sewer, or electricity. The foundation comprises discarded tires rammed with earth and stacked like blocks. Used bottles, cans and adobe mud also go into non-weight-bearing parts of the construction.

They sound very strange, I know, but in my opinion they're the most beautiful homes on the planet. And they're extremely efficient. You can grow your own food indoors and you never have to pay a utility bill. The temperature, even in the coldest of places like Northern Maine, remains consistently in the 70s indoors—without the use of any heating fuel due to the south-facing windows and thermal mass of the tires.

Before we bought the house next to the paper mill, Dan and I found and purchased 17 acres of land in the neighboring town of Grand Isle, population 512—without checking it out in person first. Who buys a house and land without checking it out first? Desperate people do. People who cannot normally get approved for conventional loans, due to credit scores that are as far south of 800 as Grand Isle is north of the equator, except in a town where the banks have an inordinate number of REOs on the books (Real Estate Owned—homes that have reverted back to the bank).

Dan and I are the perfect match for each other except in two important ways: One, neither of us copes very well when any of our children get sick and, two, we don't temper each other in the impulsivity department. I guess that's not completely true. I'm slightly less impulsive than Dan is, making and sometimes breaking my daily to-do lists. Dan, on the other hand, always just takes on each challenge as it comes to him and zealously tackles it until accomplished. I always marvel at how he's able to get done twice what I can do in the same time period, even without a to-do list.

We purchased the 17 acres on eBay with owner financing for $25,000. Incidentally, about two weeks after we gave our notice and purchased the eBay land, Dan's mom moved back home to Encinitas. But we had already committed to a new path. We had a joint vision and it was time to leave the realm of one-day and start living it, despite what other changes were happening around us.

I had fallen in love with Earthships when driving from New York City to San Diego about 12 years before I met my future husband Dan, who had been in, of all the possible vocations, the tire business for almost 30 years. It goes to show that the law of attraction is always in effect even when you're not intending it to be!

I had just completed a course at a vegetarian cooking school and was relocating to San Diego by myself. I made a point to visit Taos, New Mexico, the home of the Earthships, designed by architect Michael Reynolds. You can rent them by the night in the Greater World Community, a subdivision just outside of Taos made up entirely of Earthships. Needing a place to stay one night on my journey, I decided to treat myself to the unique experience of sleeping in one.

The moment I walked into the house, the earthy smell enveloped me. The quiet, soundproof walls bermed into the ground made me feel as if I had become a part of the earth itself. I looked out through the south-facing glass walls that separate the garden from the outside world and enjoyed the wide-open beauty and flatness of the mesa, wishing that I had someone with me to share it with, someone who would appreciate it as much as I did. This was what a house was supposed to feel like, but I needed a partner to make it feel like a home.

Chapter 3
Our Family

The girls are in school right now. Tabitha is in first grade and Willow is in Early Childhood as they call it here—the grade before kindergarten. Today is their first day back to school since the Connecticut tragedy. We put our trust in so many acquaintances and strangers all day long with the little people who are most precious to us. But as the school reminded us via email yesterday, our children are much more likely to die in some other tragedy than they are at school. They went on to list them: terminal illness, car accident, et cetera. Somehow they meant that to be comforting.

I don't find this to be a comforting thought but statistically they're right. And yet some of them have little to no chance at life from the beginning. This was our Quincy. Her genetic map was "Not of This World," to borrow a Christian window sticker phrase. Her energy was a swirling vortex that couldn't fit into human form. Not easily anyway. Like those twisted juniper trees in vortex locations like Sedona, Arizona. The swirls of energy twist the trunks as they push upward toward the sun, making them different than the other trees and, in my opinion, more beautiful.

Beauty. Some is in the eye of the beholder, some beauty is universally accepted and agreed upon as truth. Universal beauty is the type that describes my other two daughters.

Willow is four years old. She has long curly blonde hair, shockingly blue eyes as large as one of the big-eyed stuffed animals she plays with. She has a round little face and perfect upturned nose. She looks like she stepped out of the late 1800s. You could put her in a long dress and bonnet, snap a black-and-white photo of her and you would swear that she was from another time.

Willow is a fairy spirit—always dancing around and laughing with the sweetest most impish carefree child's laugh. She's also quick, smart and funny—much quicker than you would expect from one her age. One day she spread some cream cheese on a bagel for me but accidently got some of the banana bread from her plate on it. I wasn't watching her spread it but when she handed it to me I looked at it somewhat dubiously, wondering why there were brown crumbs in my white cream cheese. Sensing what I was thinking she said, "Don't worry, Mommy, it's just banana bread."

And Willow will unleash some of the funniest, most random statements. One day out of nowhere, she said, "Mommy, I think that finding a husband, building a house and hatching children is too much work!"

Willow is a generous child. If you run out of chips on your plate, she'll reach over and put some of hers on your plate.

One day, Tabitha, Willow and I were playing a board game together. Tabitha had to win, no matter what. Willow took a turn and slyly cheated. Not to help herself but to help Tabitha win. When I called her on it she burst into tears.

"I cheated! I'm s-s-sorry," she sobbed.

"It's okay, Willow," Tabitha said sweetly, encouraging her sister to continue the duplicity in order to help Tabitha reach her end goal of winning.

I tried not to laugh. They were both being themselves and learning lessons here. But it was all so dramatic for a little board game.

One evening we were having a talk at the dinner table about how babies come to be—in very general terms. Willow had been talking about a boy she knows from play group that she wants to marry one day. As we told the story of marriage and how babies are made, Willow listened intently to the whole story, paused for a moment, looked disgusted and said, "I change my mind!"

After 30 hours of trying to push her out, Tabitha came into this world a robust 10 pounds, 2 ounces. I don't know if it was a past-life issue or the broken collar bone she suffered upon descending my birth canal that caused her to have an anxious look on her face the first few months of her life as if to say, "Why am I here? I didn't agree to this!"

Tabby is a tomboy inside the body of a beauty queen. Long, straight, thick blonde hair and "rainbow eyes," as she calls them. Rainbow is her favorite "color." She has blue eyes with flecks of yellow and many other colors. Today she seems to have outgrown her worried spirit and traded it for a warrior one. I think her anxiety translated into a controlling personality, trying to fight the world—or at least her sister, competing for parental love as most siblings do. But at school she's calm, obedient, and a very good student.

Tabitha has a beautiful natural singing voice. Even her speaking voice has a musical lilt to it. The school she was attending in Julian, California was a one-room schoolhouse built in the late 1870s. In the 1930s, someone wrote a sweet little song for the school that Tabitha would often sing for us beautifully. One day Dan asked her if she could do a rap version of the song. She thought about it for a moment, then broke into the best rap I've ever heard:

"When the pears turn ripe and the walnuts fall there's a place that I long to *be,* in the green, green hills there's a green schoolhouse called Spen-cer Val-ley. Spencer Valley, Spencer Valley, Spencer Valley, we're all for you!"

It was hilarious. She did it for her teacher at school and her classmates and they all loved it so much they asked her to present it on stage at the next school performance. And she did. She wasn't nervous at all. I still wonder how she knew how to rap so perfectly. She never hears rap at home.

Tabitha is a kid's kid. Kids look up to her because she marches to her own beat. You can imagine her starring in a Disney movie, off on some adventure that would make her parents cringe as a ragtag group of kids follow her through the jungle looking for a buried treasure or a missing something.

Tabitha never admits to sleeping. "I stay awake alllll night," she declares. I suppose a warrior wouldn't want to get caught sleeping on the job. She has her softer side, too. She has the amazing ability to give people the perfect gift. She's always giving her toys away to her friends, things that she knows they would love. Tabitha even knows the right gift for grown-ups sometimes, too. Her sitter in California, Miss Linda, has an orange cat named Clifford who one day had pushed a small wooden frog toy under her stove. She hasn't been able to get it out from under there. I took the girls shopping in Julian looking for a birthday gift for Miss Linda one day and Tabitha was the one to find it.

"Let's get her this! It's a bigger frog, just like the one Clifford pushed under the stove. But it's too big to fit under there," Tabby said. Of course Linda loved it.

Tabitha had her own pre-verbal language that was kind of unique. She sounded like she was trying to speak Chinese. Because she was my first baby, and since I didn't have much experience with other children, I just assumed that's how kids sound before they can speak.

When Willow came along, she didn't have any unusual pre-verbal utterances. But when she started to form words, she sounded Italian. She would add a little something extra to some of her words. For example, the word "beard" became "beard-o" and the church bells she heard several times a day from our home became "church-a bells." It started to make me wonder about the possibility of past lives.

Tabitha said her first word when she was only 10-½ months old. One spring day in Julian, Dan made a very beautiful kite out of colored cellophane and hung it on the wall next to our kitchen table. Tabitha looked it over carefully, smiled and pointed to the kite and said "Pretty!"

At 13-½ months she counted to three right after she got a vaccination. It was bizarre. We were living on the Big Island of Hawaii in a town called Volcano. It's a town on top of the

Kilauea volcano and it is a United Nations World Heritage site because of the unique species of flora and fauna that inhabit the area.

Dan was changing her diaper in her bedroom later that evening.

"Katie, come here, you have to see this!"

I rushed into her room, frightened about what I might find. The last time Dan said, "Katie, come here, you have to see this!" I was greeted with a very unwelcome, albeit funny, surprise. That evening he gestured for me to open our front door. It was evening and I was feeling exhausted as I often do at night. I reluctantly got up off the couch and dragged my tired body across the floor, slightly annoyed at Dan for rousing me from my inert position. This house was one of those houses where you're never really sure which door is the front door. The front door really opens up onto the side yard.

I turned the doorknob and pulled the door toward me, expecting to find some rare lizard or bird as usual. As I peered out into the night, a rush of adrenaline shot through my heart: There stood the biggest black bull I'd ever seen. I suppose any untethered bull within 10 feet of you would look rather large when viewed through the lens of terror. I screamed, frightening the bull who, in turn, charged the porch causing me to scream even louder as I jumped back, slamming the door shut. "Dan! How could you?!" I scolded him as he fell onto the couch laughing.

This time there was no bull, thank goodness, just little Tabitha sitting in her diaper on the floor. Dan said, "Tabitha, count for mommy." She smiled and very slowly and deliberately said, "One, two, three." She looked back and forth from my face to Dan's and back to me again, enjoying the attention but a bit confused by all the interest.

"Oh my god! What did they put into you?" I asked, half expecting her to answer me in full sentences. She couldn't count at all that morning. Maybe it was just a coincidence. But is there ever such thing as a true coincidence?

Chapter 4
Honey, I Think the Kids are Psychic

People stop us all the time wherever we go. "Your children are sooooo beautiful!" or "They're so adorable!" It's very nice, I must admit, to get this attention. But there is a part of me that worries a little about all the focus on their looks. I was never one of those mothers that particularly wanted pretty little daughters to dress up like dolls. But now that they have chosen me to be their mother, I am so thrilled. Not because of their incredible physical beauty but because of who they are. Every single day since becoming their mother I have thanked God for them. I feel so blessed. And they're constantly cracking me up. I've been keeping a journal of quotes of all the crazy, funny things they say ever since they could speak.

But would Quincy be the black sheep in our pretty-girl family and beauty-oriented society with her cleft lip and strawberry-shaped head? Would everyone say, "Your daughters are so beautiful!" then glance uncomfortably at Quincy and say, "Well, hello there! Aren't you cute." I had no doubt that Tabitha and Willow would whole-heartedly accept and love Quincy despite any of her physical or mental limitations. It was just the rest of the world's reaction to her that made me anxious. I wasn't concerned about being judged, but I wouldn't want her feelings to get hurt accidentally by nice but unthinking or unaware acquaintances or strangers.

Willow and Tabitha are extremely lively and almost never quiet unless they're watching a TV show. When I'm out and about with Willow, people on the other side of a store can hear her when she speaks. "Willow, honey, I'm right here. I can hear you," I whisper to her, hoping she'll catch on to my tone.

As fun and lively and beautiful as they are with their own unique special talents and gifts like all children have, my girls have a little something else. A little something… extra. Something clairvoyant. Perhaps that's not the right word for it. Maybe all children have the ability, for a short time until socialization and maturation strip it from us, to see the world as it really is. It's possible that I'm just more aware of such phenomena because I'm looking for them.

On at least four different occasions, Tabitha has read minds. Once she read my mind, twice she read Dan's, and one time she apparently read our bearded dragon Daisy's mind. We were living in San Marcos, California, in Dan's parents' house and Tabitha was about two and a half years old. We had just bought a hamster for the girls for Christmas. Financially, times were very tight for us in early 2009, as they were and still are for many people around the world. Dan sometimes has what I would call a poverty consciousness. He has a very difficult time seeing himself prosperous, at least in a long-term sense.

One morning he was cooking breakfast in the kitchen and looking at our hamster, Niblet, who lived in a cage on top of the counter. He was thinking to himself a crazy thought, as we're all prone to do from time to time when we let our minds wander. "If we were ever *really* hungry, I would cook Niblet and feed him to my family."

Tabitha burst into the kitchen. "Nooooo!" she shrieked, "DON'T EAT MY HAMSTER!"

I was sitting right there at the kitchen table. "What's wrong with her?" I asked Dan accusingly. "What did you say to her?"

Dan was shocked yet had a guilty look on this face. "What? I didn't say anything!"

"Don't eat Niblet, Daddy!"

With large eyes that Dan only employs when he's really, really spooked, "I swear I didn't say anything, Katie. I... " he paused for a moment, looking embarrassed. "I *thought* it, though."

"You *thought* you wanted to eat the kids' hamster? There's no meat on a hamster. Why wouldn't you think about eating the dog instead?"

"That's my dog!" Dan declared protectively.

"And that's their hamster!" I teased him, simultaneously amused and in awe of my older daughter's new talent.

Another mindreading incident occurred when Dan was out of the country in Dubai, United Arab Emirates, working on an export tire deal. Besides working in the retail side of the tire industry, Dan makes most of our income from brokering export tire deals. He arranges shipments of tires via containers all over the world.

I was trying to entertain the girls while he was away and give them some leeway, more than I usually would. One afternoon Tabitha insisted on putting both of our bearded dragon lizards into a plastic tote so she could play with them. So I let her. No problem. After about an hour it was time to go over to Miss Linda's house for a visit, so I told Tabby to put the lizards back in their cage.

"No, don't worry, Mommy, it will be fine," she assured me.

I sort of doubted this but the tote seemed rather deep and the sides were slippery. Unless one of them gave the other a leg up, I didn't really see how they could easily escape.

As any parent who has been left alone for a long period of time with their children—especially when you're not used to it—you know that you pick your battles. So I let the lizards remain in the tote. We walked over to Linda's and she and I talked for about an hour while the girls played with her cats and her stash of toys that she keeps for her grandkids and her babysitting charges. When it was about time to go, Tabitha panicked.

"Daisy has escaped! We have to go home now!"

"Tabitha," I cajoled, "she's probably fine. You were right; that tote was really deep. And if anyone was going to escape, it's probably Rocky because he's bigger and stronger."

She kept insisting that we go home immediately. So, again, to appease her we did. Sure enough, we returned to find Rocky in the tote—and Daisy was missing. About an hour later Tabitha found Daisy hiding under the china cabinet perfectly fine.

Willow has her clairvoyant moments, too. I had mentioned to the girls that Dan and I would be trying to have another baby but that there were no guarantees because mommy and daddy are a bit older. I probably didn't have to mention this to them at all but I was excited at the possibility of having another baby and I wanted to gauge their reaction. Dan and I were 43 at the time and I was suffering a bit from what I thought was psoriatic arthritis. It's basically an autoimmune disorder where the immune system attacks healthy joints and other tissues of the body.

Seven years earlier I had a bout of similar symptoms and had a battery of tests done but no doctors could diagnose what I had. I read a book by natural health expert Gary Null, who recommended a few ancient herbs to remedy the situation: cayenne pepper, boswellia, devil's claw and some liquid chlorophyll. I did this for about two weeks and all symptoms disappeared. I went on with my active lifestyle and didn't think about it again. I had been going through a tough time and I just thought it was my body reacting to that stress.

About seven years later similar but slightly different symptoms emerged. I tried the herbs but no luck this time. In fact, it seemed to make the symptoms worse. So as most people do, I started searching the Internet. That's a great way to misdiagnose and scare oneself to death! Nevertheless, I found a study by the National Institutes of Health that claimed that most women who get pregnant have a complete remission of symptoms from psoriatic arthritis.

"Should we do it?" I asked Dan. "I would love another baby, you know that."

"Sure," said my impulsive husband. "Let's go for it."

"We're not too old?" I asked, really wanting reassurance from him that I wasn't too old.

"If it's meant to be, it will happen," he said.

"Really?" I asked, apprehensive yet excited. "Okay. Let's just give it a two-month window and see what happens. We'll leave it up to God or the universe. I don't want to force things."

I had had a nagging feeling for the previous few years that there was one more spirit that wanted to be born. Just one. I thought about it a lot. Was this just my subconscious desire to have another baby to love and love me or was there really someone else who wanted to come into our family? Did I want to have one more child because I was the oldest of three and that family size felt right to me?

I had a vague memory of getting a psychic reading at a New York City street fair years earlier. I remember the reader was an Asian woman with unusual fingernails. She had neatly filed her nails into sharp points and she used her nails to pinpoint mysterious numbers in what looked to be some kind of star chart book.

"You are going to have three children. Three girls," she told me, eyes wide. At the time I was single and in my early 30s and I thought to myself, "Yeah, right, *I'm* going to have three kids. I'd better get busy!" I could never figure out why her eyes looked so large and spooked. Maybe she was reading about Quincy but didn't want to say?

Chapter 5
Shagging Dan

Getting pregnant was never a problem for us; keeping the babies was. We had a couple of miscarriages in the first 8 weeks. Our pattern was miscarriage, baby, miscarriage, baby.

Though Dan and I are not conventional or religious people, we definitely consider ourselves spiritually oriented. We met on Match.com in our 37th year of life. Not being one to wait for what I want, I saw his profile on Match and contacted him right away. Dan is very attractive with piercing brown eyes, a large masculine nose, thick brown caterpillar-like eyebrows, beautiful smile, and untamed curly brown hair. Some of the photos showed him clean cut with short hair and surfer clothing; others showed his wilder side with long hair and wearing a leather motorcycle jacket while sitting atop his Harley.

My first impression was that he seemed to be the perfect blend of good guy and bad boy—a rare find. After I got to know him I learned that he's not bad at all, just kind of wild, untamable and slightly reckless. And, most importantly, extremely loyal and loving to me.

His profile also had a photo of him with his sister at some family event and a picture of his puppy dog. In the section where you get to write about what's important to you he outlined his goals. "I worked with mentally handicapped kids in Alaska and I was a foster parent. I want to open a ranch with horses for handicapped adults and children."

After I read that, I was hooked. "Let's get together and play sometime," I emailed. He took that as I meant it—let's go play on the beach, goof around—just play like kids. He called me that night.

The moment I heard his voice on the phone, I knew that at the very least we'd become best friends. And to this day we are.

"Let's get together for coffee," I suggested confidently, excited to meet him and having the feeling that the excitement was mutual. I didn't like to waste time on the phone with people only to be disappointed in person when there's no chemistry.

The next day Dan called me with some bad news. "Katie, I'm so sorry but my car has broken down and I can't come pick you up. I'm working on it right now but I don't know how long it's going to take me to fix it."

"Oh, that's a bummer. I hope you get it fixed soon. But it's no problem. We'll do it another time," I said cheerfully, hiding my disappointment.

I was hanging out at the local hipster coffee house at the time when he called. I love the ambience of these places, but I always wish that I could just be an unobserved voyeur sitting in the corner, hiding my own self-conscious un-hipness.

Normally I would wonder if I was getting the blow off, but for some reason I believed Dan. I still felt some kind of connection to him and I figured if it was meant to happen, it will. Anyone who has ever tried online dating knows that it can be a numbers game sometimes and you need to have a tough skin. You meet a lot of people who are nice but it can take a while before you're lucky enough to find someone truly in sync with you.

As I carried my latte away from the counter looking for a seat in the corner, I clumsily tripped over nothing and spilled some of my coffee on the floor.

"Let me help you with that," said an attractive male stranger who was seated alone.

This would have been the perfect opportunity to get to know a random cute guy. But right as he bent over to wipe up my mess, I had an urgent, overwhelming feeling: "I've got to go pick up Dan—now!"

I thanked the handsome stranger for his help and quickly scooted away out of his earshot to call Dan.

"Hey, it's Katie. What if I come pick you up?"

"That would be fantastic!"

"Ok, cool. See you in 20 minutes."

"There's a coffee shop right near my place that we can go to and play chess, if you want. I'll bring the board," he said.

I pulled up to his house. It was a simple one-story well-maintained house in a slightly declining older neighborhood. Dan hoisted himself up from under his car and made a beeline for my pickup truck. He opened the passenger door and hopped right in.

"Thanks for picking me up," he smiled.

He was very cute but I suddenly felt a little nervous that this stranger got right into my vehicle before we even said hello. But nevertheless we headed for the coffee shop about five minutes way.

As I had expected, we really hit it off and had a fun time hanging out and playing together. He was fun and easy to talk to. To this day, though, I can't remember if I beat him or if he beat me at chess because I definitely wasn't focusing on the board!

Three weeks later we got engaged and three months after the first day we met we married. The day before we got engaged, Dan said to me, "I want to take you out for a special dinner." This was our first nice dinner out, and for some reason I had the feeling he was going to propose. There was no reason for me to think this except that I knew we were moving quickly and that we both felt we were right together.

So I bought a new dress for the occasion, just in case my intuition was correct, and spent extra time fixing myself up. I also had the feeling that he was going to take me to the Chart House in Cardiff-by-the-Sea, a suburb of San Diego. I had no solid reason to think this either. In our three-week courtship, we had never even discussed this restaurant. I just kind of knew.

And I was right. That evening we were engaged at The Chart House.

We moved in together right away into my small Carlsbad apartment where I quickly became pregnant. We knew we wanted to be together forever and have children and we were also realistic about our ages. We were both eager to start a family as soon as possible. When I became pregnant, we decided to move into a larger apartment in the same complex to make room for the three of us.

Our homemade wedding invitations said "Dan and Katie are a) Getting Married b) Having a Baby or c) All of the Above?" with "C" circled. Within a week of sending out the invites, I had a miscarriage. A missed miscarriage, I think they call it. That's where the baby doesn't have a heartbeat but your body hasn't expelled the embryo yet. I was so disappointed. Always one to go the natural route first, I decided to wait a bit to see what would happen. I figured my body would know what to do. It didn't. A week later I had a dilation and curettage (D&C) surgery.

After the surgery, I worried about my ability to bear children. What if I couldn't have children with this man I loved? I had also had a miscarriage when I was 22 during my first marriage.

We put the baby idea on the back burner for a while. There were some pressing issues we had to deal with first. Due to some job shifts and the increase in rent, money troubles hit us hard and we were having great difficulty making the rent. But despite our troubles and worries, it was mostly a happy time because we were newly in love.

As a big fan of craigslist, Dan finds it relaxing to cruise the things for sale and freebies categories just to see what's out there. About a week after the surgery, Dan was on craigslist in the vehicles section and found something intriguing.

"Hey, Katie, listen to this: There's a 1978 Dodge Sportsman RV in the free section. It says, 'You come pick up and remove.' What if we got it and fixed it up? We could live in it rent free. Then we could save up for our wedding and maybe eventually even save for a house. What do you think?"

I was a bit doubtful at first so we debated it back and forth. "Where would we put our stuff?"

"Storage."

"It would be amazing to live rent free," I said, trying to talk myself into it. But as one who is usually up for an adventure, it didn't take me long to decide. "Let's do it!"

We drove to Los Angeles that day to check it out. It was parked next to a beautiful house in an older but upscale suburban neighborhood. Replete with green shag carpet and 8-track tapes, it had sat there in the exact same spot for 25 plus years like a time capsule. The woman who was getting rid of it had left it there so long in order to humor her husband. But when he passed away, the echoes of fun family memories made her sad; now she just wanted it gone.

The RV was laden with rat feces, mold, and water damage. It was probably better suited for a landfill. But here we were all the way up in LA and excited for a new project and committing ourselves to the challenge.

Dan, not known for his deliberation skills, jumped into the project and jerry-rigged it to start. The owner told us that the engine hadn't been started in over 25 years. Dan convinced the landscapers who were working next door to use their truck as a brace to keep the RV from careening out of control down the steep driveway. Dan tied an old tire with a rope to their tailgate, using it as a bumper between the pickup truck and the several-ton RV.

As I feared, the RV was too heavy, causing the tire to slip off and putting a big dent in the pickup truck tailgate as it bottomed out at the end of the driveway, sending sparks flying into the air. Fortunately, the propane tank didn't explode. We offered to fix the landscapers' tailgate, but they told us not to bother.

I drove our car back home and Dan drove the RV by himself from LA to San Diego *on tires that were 25+ years old*. When he arrived at home, it wouldn't start again. The fuel lines were completely clogged. How he got it to San Diego safely is a complete mystery to me.

After a few weeks of some very hard work, we renovated the interior but kept the green shag carpet and dubbed it "The Shag Mobile." Dan's mom sewed 1970s-style flower power seat cushions and I made fuzzy blue curtains and painted flowers on the outside of the vehicle. We put a lava lamp in the corner to complete the theme. Together we moved all of our stuff out of the new apartment, put most of it into storage and the rest into The Shag. By the end of the project we were exhausted.

But we soon recovered and enjoyed the carefree life of people who live under the radar. During the day we parked at the beach and had romantic sunset dinners from our new kitchen table, which also doubled as our bed. After dark we would drive into unmanned beach campgrounds and dump our sewage in their receptacle and fill up with fresh water. After we were all set for the evening, we'd drive to a vacant lot near the Coaster railroad tracks by the beach and sleep cuddled up and happy.

But our carefree, rent-free life turned into more of a pain as time went on. Moving your "house" constantly to avoid getting ticketed is not an easy way to live. By no means were we the only people in San Diego doing this. In fact, there's a whole subculture of people living this way. It is usually older retired and/or broke men but sometimes it is hippie couples or families trying to stay off the streets.

But the city made it tough for us folks on purpose. Otherwise, there would have been huge communities of people living in RVs or trucks in this warm-year-round city. It turns out you can't stay parked anywhere for a 24-hour period. And most businesses do not want an RV parked in their lots either. Wal-Mart will let you stay parked for a few days but then you have to move on. In other parts of the country campers are welcome to stay much longer in their parking lots, I imagine in the hopes of needing to run into Wally World for constant replenishment of supplies.

While still living in The Shag Mobile, we had a small wedding ceremony at Moonlight Beach in Encinitas. We had about 30 friends and family present. My oldest friend, Edmund, became an ordained minister on the Internet in order to perform our ceremony. Dan and I wrote our own vows to each other. The ceremony commenced with Elvis's song "Only Fools Rush In."

The ceremony was held at sunset and performed Quaker style. One aspect to this is after the "I Do's," you invite all of your family and friends to give their words of wisdom about love and marriage, if they want to. And, to our surprise, they did.

At the end, everyone was invited to sign a contract, witnessing our union and promising to help us see it through.

Dan and I have been together for nearly eight years and we're closer now than when we got married. We're truly best friends. Strangers and acquaintances often tell us how "cute" we are together or how much love we seem to have for each other. Years after our wedding, I was getting eyeglasses at Costco with our younger daughter in tow. Dan was helping me pick out frames.

"Are you two newlyweds?" the woman behind the counter asked.

I was kind of puzzled because Willow was standing next to us. Of course, she could have been one of ours or both of ours after getting married later. But if one were to make assumptions from the outside, you'd probably assume that we were a family and that we were not newlyweds. It was the second time that week we had heard that comment.

"No, why?" I asked.

"Well, he's so sweet and complimenting you; he's so helpful and attentive. It just seemed like you are newlyweds." That's the kind of person Dan is.

Chapter 6

Just Being

In life I've always striven so hard to achieve and make things happen. I'm hardworking and I'd like to think that I'm clever and inventive, though recently I've come to doubt this due to my lack of great financial success. I know my standards are high and my level of success may seem high to some and non-existent to others. In any event, although I do believe in the law of attraction, my first instinct is to "go for it"—run after what I want. I've learned that this is not always a great policy and quite often very unproductive.

From time to time I like to do the *I Ching* (also called The Book of Changes, an ancient book of divination originating in China). It seems to me that most of the responses you get from flipping the coins advise you to "be still" or "don't act," or something about following in the footsteps of the Sage. I've never found the I Ching's advice to be easy but it always seems like good advice no matter what the toss of the coins bring.

Since Quincy came into my life, I've come to realize that we all affect many more people in our lives by being who we are rather than doing what we believe will bring us love, happiness, recognition or admiration. I can tell by how people react to Dan and me, our loving relationship, and how they react to us as a family that we are affecting them in a positive way. Giving people hope of how it can be, how love and family were meant to be.

Not that we're the perfect family. We yell at our kids too much—especially Tabitha, the more challenging one. But overall I know that when we are just being ourselves, we are having an impact on our little world around us.

One day I was going for a walk along a bike path in a suburban neighborhood in California. It was a bit chilly out, just cool enough for a light jacket or heavy sweater. I passed by an elderly woman who was walking very slowly as she was propped up by a slightly younger but much healthier woman. The caretaker was singing to the elderly woman. It was one of the most beautiful voices I've ever heard. They were both completely unaware of my observing them and of the impact they had on me. If I had heard that same voice in a concert hall, I doubt I would have been as affected. But I could see and feel the beauty of the love and comfort the caretaker was giving. I think we all affect and influence each other the most when we're not trying to.

Chapter 7

Quincy

A few days before I knew I was pregnant, I was sitting on my bed with Willow on my lap as I dried her hair with a towel. She turned and looked at me with a scrunched up nose and said with surprise, "Mommy, there's a baby in your belly!"

"Really?" I asked. I know they're not always right, but I never dismiss my children's intuition.

She nodded. "It's a girl and her name is Quincy."

Willow has always been quick to name her dolls and stuffed animals and she usually comes up with very creative names. But how she knew I was having a baby girl and where she heard the name Quincy, I don't know. The only place that I could think of where she may have heard the name would have been on the *Little Einsteins* TV show, but she had only seen it with her big sister once or twice when she was still a baby.

I believe Quincy really was her name, as a gifted psychic in Sedona would demonstrate to us a few months later.

As I said, I was trying to get pregnant so I knew that it was a possibility, but I certainly didn't feel pregnant yet. No sore boobs, no bloating, no queasiness. The next day after Willow's prognostication I came down with a violent flu.

"This completely sucks," I told Dan as he held my hair out of my face as I bent over the porcelain. "But the good news is that for some reason my arthritis symptoms are gone."

"You're probably pregnant," Dan stated matter-of-factly.

"No, I doubt it. This definitely feels like the flu."

Well, it didn't occur to me that I could have the flu *and* be pregnant! When the flu abated, I took a pregnancy test a few days after my missed period and Willow and Dan were right—I was pregnant!

"Told you. I have powerful seed," Dan said proudly, puffing out his chest.

It's the ego talking but I was kind of proud, too, that I could get pregnant so easily at 43. Like I have anything to do with it really. Two months is all it took, just like my timeline. It must be "meant to be." Or is that just what we say when things go our way or to comfort ourselves when they don't? Dan and I often debate the concept of predestination or fate. He seems more certain than I am about this theory.

The pregnancy seemed to go along as most of them do for me; some nausea in the first trimester, extreme fatigue, the usual. Ever since Tabitha's birth I've resolved to eat moderately when pregnant. I gained 65 pounds with her and she was born 10 pounds 2 ounces. I'm somewhat tall, 5', 8", but my frame is slight and my hips are narrow (normally I'm 125 to 130 pounds). I had a miserable time in the last month of pregnancy with her, carrying all of that extra weight. And it took me months to recover from a third-degree tear. If you don't know what that is, do yourself a favor and don't look it up, especially if you've never had children before and plan to.

I was determined to have a natural birth this time. It was a dream of mine to give birth quietly at home in a birthing tub with my loved ones around me. But because we were living in Julian, which was about an hour and 15 minutes from the nearest hospital, we were leaning toward having her at a birthing center down in the city. In any case, until we decided for certain, we were going to have my prenatal care there.

So all four of us piled into our car and drove downtown for the first ultrasound. The machine there was very old and outdated due to lack of funding at the birth center, but it was adequate for most ultrasounds of healthy babies.

The ultrasound tech and her partner were taking forever to do the test. But I wasn't too apprehensive because I could see

Quincy on the monitor. "Look, girls, see the baby?" They thought it was pretty cool. But being wiggly young kids, they were becoming a bit unmanageable after spending too much time in a very small room.

"Are we almost done?" I asked.

"Almost. Just a couple more measurements. Do you want to know the sex?"

"Yes," Dan and I said in unison.

"It's… a baby girl!"

"Willow, you were right! That's amazing," I said. She looked pleased.

The ultrasound reading dragged on and I began to get an uneasy feeling in my stomach. Dan and I were both 43 and we knew there could be some risk. But she looked so beautiful and perfect on the monitor, to me. I was pretty sure there was nothing to worry about.

"So how is everything?" I asked nervously.

"Um, well, we're going to recommend you get another ultrasound. A level 2. Our equipment is very old and some things are—unclear."

"Like what?" Dan snapped.

"Well, she seems to have a very small stomach. And we can't see the tube connecting to the stomach. And her head is odd shaped. She has an echo foci on her heart, which could indicate something like Downs but we don't know for sure."

When I heard the term "echo foci" I bristled. This was something we heard when I was pregnant with Willow. We got the level 2 ultrasound then and it was not resolved. We were told by the impassive level 2 doctor, "Could be a sign of Downs or maybe not. Won't know until she comes out. Unless you want to get an amnio." I knew in my heart that she was fine and it pissed me off that they were trying to scare me with this vague information. My brother's son had the same reading and he was born very healthy, too.

The tech at the birth center ushered us out of the tiny ultrasound room into a smaller midwife room.

"So what does this mean? Anything to worry about?" I asked.

"No, I don't think so. We're just being ultra cautious. Our equipment is out of date," said the midwife.

We returned home from the ultrasound and I pondered it for a few days. What did it all mean? Should I be afraid or just brush it off? I went about my weekly routine, taking Willow to story time at our local library in Julian. I'd pack a backpack and, if time allowed, we'd walk the half mile through town to the library, greeting friends and familiar faces along the way. Willow had her own routine. When we passed town hall, I'd have to pause for a few minutes, acting as her spotter, as she hopped up on a retaining wall, putting one foot in front of the other, traversing it like a tight rope walker.

Julian is a wonderful flourishing rural community in the mountains of San Diego County. Full of wild life, such as turkeys, deer and the occasional rattlesnake and mountain lion, and good people, it was close to the idyllic setting for Dan and me to raise our girls. Julian is rich in history and has been carefully preserved as a historic town. Built during the gold rush of the late 1800s, it still thrives today as a tourist destination. Today, people mostly visit for the natural beauty, historic buildings and apple pie or apple picking.

There's a wealth of creative types in this area, from writers to artists as well as a bevy of retirees from various backgrounds. The only drawbacks of living there were major threats of fire every summer and fall, the possibility of rattlesnake bites in the summer, and the extraordinarily high cost of living. Our dream to own a farm, or even just a modest house, had thus far been unattainable for us in Julian.

As with most places where there is a chasm between the haves and the have-nots, there is also a lot of class division or snobbery. Dan and I have lived in many places and in towns where folks don't drive luxury cars, and there's not a lot of comparing or showing off of what one has. Although it was less pronounced than in the coastal towns of San Diego, Julian unfortunately was not one of these places.

All my mom friends attended story time and our babysitter and good friend, Miss Linda, a retired teacher, volunteered each week to read to the little ones who were not quite old enough for school. I went about my week after the ultrasound as if everything was fine, but in the back of my mind there was a nagging doubt. In fact, I had a nagging doubt about this pregnancy from the moment of conception. The doubt was based on the reasonable question, "Am I too old to bear a healthy child?"

Dan and I started having children later in life. Tabitha was born when I was 38; Willow was born in my 40th year. The age issue never bothered me at all—until now. Was it my actual chronological age of 43 that was bothering me or did I have psychic or intuitive insight that not all was well in my womb? I fully believe that we all have access to much more knowledge than our five senses give us. But relatively few people know how or allow themselves to be in touch with this intuitive knowingness. And even fewer people are consistently able to access this power, either through practice or with a natural innate third eye channel that has no barriers.

"Dan, I don't think another ultrasound is going to make any difference. Their equipment is just old. And a lot of people don't even get ultrasounds in the natural health community anyway. They're somewhat invasive and you can tell Quincy didn't like it. She kept moving away from the probe."

"It's up to you, Sweetie. I'll support whatever you decide. You know your baby."

There was a persistent feeling inside of me that I was trying to ignore that said "go get the level 2." But I canceled the second ultrasound anyway and let it go, continuing on with my pregnancy into my 21st week. Then I received a disturbing phone call.

"Hello, my name is C_____. I'm a midwife with the birth center. Is there a reason you canceled your level 2 ultrasound?"

"Yes," I said somewhat taken aback. "The midwife didn't seem to think there was anything to worry about and said that your equipment was just old. We went through this before with our younger daughter and she turned out to be just fine."

"I strongly urge you to see the level 2 specialist, Dr. Z. He's very good and caring. And he's a perinatologist, specializing in problem pregnancies."

"Problem?" I questioned nervously.

"Mrs. Marsh, your ultrasound shows some possible serious complications. Your baby may have trisomy 18 or Downs.

This is not something we are equipped to handle at our birth center. If your baby does have one of these issues, then you need hospital care."

Piercing panic coursed through my body like lightning. There could not be something wrong with my baby. I was 21 weeks pregnant and I felt her moving around every day. My belly was quite distended at this point and I was wearing maternity clothes. I saw her on the ultrasound. She looked fine to me. She had a beautiful profile with the cutest little pug nose. Other than the arthritis getting worse instead of getting better like I had hoped, this felt like a normal pregnancy.

As Christmas was approaching I decided to be brave and get the level 2 ultrasound. It was the responsible thing to do, I decided. Dan and I drove to his parents' house in Encinitas to drop the girls off.

"We don't know when we'll be back, but sometime this evening."

Since we rarely had time alone together, we decided to go out for Indian food at Passage to India before the ultrasound. This restaurant catered our wedding on Moonlight Beach six years earlier. I also ate there the day before I gave birth to Tabitha in hopes that the spicy food would coax her out. This was a place that delighted our taste buds while also offering familiarity and comfort before we faced what could be devastating news. I definitely felt anxious but denial was the first defense.

"I'm sure she's fine. She looked great. The ultrasound machine was just old. I'm sure we'll get some positive reassuring news," I told Dan, trying to calm my nerves.

"I'm sure you're right. Why didn't that place update their equipment anyway? It's crazy to make us nervous over nothing. But whatever happens, I'm here for you, Katie Bear."

I kept thinking God wouldn't do this twice to someone. It's like getting struck twice by lightning—it doesn't happen.

Then I remembered a friend of ours in Julian who was actually struck by lightning twice and lived. Years ago Dan's first wife had an ultrasound in the seventh month of pregnancy.

"As you can see," said the doctor casually, "there is no heartbeat. So we'll need to schedule an induction tomorrow to abort the fetus."

Shocked and angry, Dan said to the doctor, "Well, it would help if you would plug the machine in and turn it on!" This was how they were informed of the death of their baby. The induction proceeded and he got to hold his little girl before letting her go.

That experience profoundly affected Dan's faith in God and his spirituality. It made him question and even doubt everything he had believed in. At the time Dan had been attending a church that emphasized faith; they preached that if you have enough faith in faith itself, God can and will do anything for you. After his daughter died, it made him doubt God's love.

After we finished our delightful lunch, we drove to the posh prenatal care office, parked and went in. We sat in the waiting room for over an hour. The office was decorated for Christmas but I just wasn't in the Christmas spirit. I sat there waiting, realizing I was totally unprepared for the ultrasound. I had forgotten to pack, and drink, a bottle of water, not to mention breath mints. I reeked of Indian food and in this lovely office I felt very self-conscious about it. We were finally escorted into an exam room and a pretty blonde tech performed the 3D ultrasound.

"Wait, let me check something. Looks like your cervix is too open but I'll have the doctor take another look," she said cheerfully.

"What would that mean?" I asked.

"Not too much, except you'd have to go on bed rest immediately."

"Oh my God! I have two little girls and no family to help. How could we handle that?!"

"Well, I had to do it during my last pregnancy. Friends and family just pitched in and made it work. It was hard, though," she agreed.

Later we found out from a nurse friend of ours that this tech had no right to make any diagnoses. It turns out she was wrong and needlessly agitated me about that aspect of the ultrasound.

"Let me call in Dr. Z. I just want to have him check over my readings. Make yourself comfortable," she said as she quickly left the room.

Lying flat on my back with my bulging belly and full bladder, I considered how this would be possible, making myself comfortable. And when was the last time I was truly comfortable anyway, I wondered. Dr. Z soon entered our dimly lit room and greeted us warmly.

"I'm so sorry to be sniffling. I have terrible allergies." A nurse followed him in and handed him a present from one of his patients. It seemed like it was something that happened to him often and my impression was that his sniffling seemed to be more about emotion than about allergies.

As he proceeded to measure my belly, he kept saying, "You guys are awesome, you're so wonderful. You're beautiful people." Countless times he repeated this, praising us as if we were the most amazing patients he had ever seen. We had a brief discussion about what we knew so far about why we needed a level 2 ultrasound.

"Well, here we do see some abnormal shape to the chambers of the heart. And she appears to have a cleft lip or palate. I can't tell which at this point. And her stomach is very, very small and doesn't seem to be connected to the esophagus.

And her head is a bit strawberry shaped. You're beautiful, amazing people, by the way."

"Why?" I blurted out. "Because we're not freaking out over what you're telling us?"

"No," he seemed a little hurt. "You are just wonderful people. Katie, do me a favor. Please get dressed and you and Dan meet me in my office next door. Take your time."

"Ok," I whispered.

After moving into the next room, this kind doctor laid it all out for us. I wondered how someone so sweet and sensitive could do this kind of work every day. He didn't seem to have the detachment needed for self-survival. You could tell that he deeply cared for his patients and their babies.

"So what is our angel's name?" asked Dr. Z.

"Quincy," I told him. "Our daughter Willow named her."

"Quincy, I love that name. Our angel, Quincy, has some health problems. As far as we can tell from the ultrasound she either has Down's Syndrome or trisomy 18. Are you familiar with these?"

I remembered an old episode of Oprah about a little boy named Eliot. The mother found out two months before he was born that he had Trisomy 18. She continued the pregnancy and gave birth to him. (Go to YouTube or Oprah.com and look up 99 Balloons: A Tribute to Eliot to see the amazing video.) Every day he lived they held a birthday party for him and took tons of pictures. Then one day when he was 99 days old he took a sudden downturn and died. It was a very touching video and I remember crying when I saw it. Of course I cried. Everybody cried. It was just so beautiful how positive the parents were and how much they celebrated every second of that baby's life.

"I've heard of it," I told Dr. Z honestly, "but I don't know much about trisomy 18." I was feeling more shock than panic at this point. It was sort of like hearing about someone else's tragedy; I felt disassociated.

"Well, trisomy 18, also called Edwards Syndrome, is a chromosomal disorder where the genetic map of the baby is incompatible with life from the very beginning. It occurs in about 1 in 6,000 live births. But about half of babies diagnosed with T18 are stillbirths. And less than 10 percent of those who survive birth live to see their first birthday. Some do grow into teens and adulthood, but it's very rare. And they have many health problems their entire lives. They usually can't speak or walk or crawl. They have to eat through a feeding tube and have their diapers changed and live in a wheelchair. I think it's most likely that Quincy is T18 rather than Downs. But we won't know for sure unless we get an amniocentesis."

He paused for a moment to look at our chart. I kept listening to him silently, feeling completely hopeless and deflated.

"Now you're about 22 weeks. At this point some parents would choose to terminate after confirmation by an amniocentesis. Others would carry to term. It's totally up to you and I'll be here to support you. We can stay here and discuss this all night, if you'd like. I'm in no hurry."

"No, we need time to digest this," I said, wanting to get the hell out of there. "Let's schedule the amnio so we know exactly what we're facing," I said, still in shock.

To my surprise, the doctor and his assistant moved very quickly to schedule the amnio. Within five minutes they had an appointment for me for first thing in the morning.

Later I realized the reason they acted so quickly is that most parents choose to terminate after getting the results of the amnio, so I suppose they felt it was important to get it done as fast as possible.

"Thank you, Dr. Z, for your forthrightness." I gave him a hug, too numb to even cry yet but truly appreciating his directness.

Dan was tearing up. "Thank you, Dr. Z. We'll see you tomorrow."

"Thank you for being such wonderful, beautiful people. I wish all my patients were like you," he said.

After gathering the kids from my in-laws' house and heading up the mountain to Julian, that's when Dan and I had the termination discussion and I felt the kick.

"Whoa," I exclaimed as I clutched my belly with both hands, startled and a bit frightened by the sudden violent movement. After a moment I got the feeling that she wasn't in any physical danger.

"Dan, feel this!" I whispered excitedly, trying not to wake up the kids. He removed his right hand from the steering wheel and allowed me to guide it to the correct spot on my belly.

Wide-eyed, I turned awkwardly in my seat to face him. "She *hears* me. She *knows* what I'm saying!"

"Well, that's your answer about termination, right?"

"I couldn't do it anyway. I just wanted to talk about it, find out your thoughts." Although the truth is I was considering it for a moment, the panicked fearful side of me. What if she dies inside of me while I'm carrying her? Could I handle that? It was a very likely scenario, if the ultrasound was correct.

Then there was another factor also guided by fear. I was beginning to feel like a ball in a pinball machine bouncing around off of different points each labeled with a different and more abhorrent fear.

"I can't have another abortion. I still have mixed feelings about it and that was over 11 years ago," I said.

Chapter 8

Abortion

It is something I've thought about a lot over the years. Today, I still consider myself "pro choice," but I do feel it's not a choice that should be made lightly or if the woman sees any other option for herself. The main reason I'm pro choice has to do with privacy and safety. It is a very private decision for a woman and/or a woman and her partner to make. In my opinion, a government has no business being involved and making it medically hazardous for women who choose to terminate. But that said, I feel you don't need to be "pro life" to choose life.

I was living with my boyfriend, Tom, at the time and I was on the pill. I also took a course of antibiotics one month for a persistent urinary tract infection and the doctor didn't inform me that I could get pregnant while on the pill and taking antibiotics. Maybe this is common knowledge to most women but it wasn't to me at the time. I got pregnant. And this person was not someone I felt inclined to spend the next week with much less share parenting with him for the rest of my life.

I told him I was pregnant. He was happy about it at first but as the stress of the pregnancy fell on him, he started acting erratically. He'd slap me very hard on the butt when joking around. He'd avoid eye contact with me and he'd come home at odd hours.

One afternoon when I confronted him about what I suspected was a return to heavy drinking, he avoided eye contact with me again while pretending to play with my cat on the floor.

"Are you drinking again, Tom?"

"No, I'm not," he said, right before vomiting on top of my cat. Poor kitty.

As it turns out, he was doing a lot more than just drinking. Cocaine and who knows what else. If you've ever seen the movie *Leaving Las Vegas* with Nicholas Cage, it is no understatement to say Tom was this type of self-destructive and suicidal alcoholic.

A couple of days later when he was at work renovating a house down the street, I packed a bag of clothes, put my cat in his carrier and sneaked out. I got on a plane and went back East to see what, if any, kind of friend and family support I would have to help me raise a baby. As I suspected, there was no support. Friends were well meaning, but they were very busy with their lives. So with no job, no money, no partner and no family support, I felt completely overwhelmed. I called an adoption agency and told them the story.

"That's fine, we'd love to start the paperwork for you. But you have to have the father sign the papers, too, giving up his rights."

I couldn't believe I had to communicate with him again. Reluctantly, I called Tom. I'm surprised I could understand what he was saying between slurs. He was at the beginning of a month-long bender.

"Tom, you have to sign these papers. I'm giving up the baby for adoption." At this point I was about seven weeks along and breaking out in the worst case of hives all over my belly, I assumed from all the stress.

"No way, no how. You're not doing this. I'll fight you all the way. I'll raise the baby myself!"

I froze. This was too much. I could no longer fight the world. That's when I made the decision to end the pregnancy. I told my 80-year-old Catholic grandmother, affectionately known as Little G in my family, about my decision and bless her sweetness, she said to me softly, "I can take the baby for you." Due to her frailty and age, I knew she wouldn't even be able to babysit much less take care of a baby full time.

I was depressed about it for a few months afterwards as I recovered from the abortion and the whole ordeal with Tom.

But then life went on and I didn't think much about it. It wasn't until years later when Willow was born that I felt some strange guilt and regret. I still to this day have no idea why it bubbled up then. But it was there and it plagued me. I thought about it a lot and finally came to realize or rationalize that our lives are made up of good acts and bad decisions, and I didn't feel that my whole life in whatever afterworld exists would be judged and hinge on that one act if our creator is a loving entity.

In a way what I went through with Quincy feels like my salvation or redemption for the abortion. In other words, I have the sense that I've paid my dues. I was raised Catholic and it's so hard to escape notions of salvation and sin, even though I'm decidedly not Catholic now for many reasons.

The only organized religion that I've ever gibed with is Self-Realization Fellowship, also known simply as SRF. I would still attend services at SRF now if there was a temple near my home. Here is a description of it from their website:

"Paramahansa Yogananda founded Self-Realization Fellowship in 1920 to make available the universal teachings of Kriya Yoga, a sacred spiritual science originating millenniums ago in India.

"These nonsectarian teachings embody a complete philosophy and way of life for achieving all-round success and well-being, as well as methods of meditation for achieving life's ultimate goal—union of the soul with Spirit (God)."

I like SRF because of the heavy focus on meditation and having a personal relationship with your creator. You don't need a church to be spiritual; it's just there for guidance, if desired, and fellowship.

If I could turn back time, would I still have made the same decision and had the abortion? It's hard to say. Maybe I would have realized my own strength and ability to pull my life back together and handle a baby. But if I had the opportunity to go back in time, the smart thing to do would have been to not tell Tom about the baby and to tell the adoption agency that I didn't know who the father was. Deceitful, for sure, but it would have been the only way to make adoption possible.

Or better yet, if I could rewind time, I would go far enough back to skip that relationship altogether. Even though I know that we are a collection of all of our life experiences, especially the very difficult ones, I still can't help but feel that I could have lived better without having had that particular life experience. But, then, without that painful experience years ago, would I have chosen differently when Quincy came into my life?

I hesitated about writing about my abortion in this book. I could have easily told Quincy's story without including that experience. My fear is that you, dear reader, will judge me as harshly as I have judged myself at times, especially if you have never had the experience yourself or if it clashes with your religious or moral beliefs.

But I felt it was important to tell this story to juxtapose two different paths taken by one woman given two different situations. I also wanted to show that no matter what your spiritual or moral beliefs are, if you are a pregnant woman who is told your baby is not likely to live and if she does she won't be healthy, as long as you feel safe and supported by people around you, you can survive this. I did.

But the choice is uniquely and personally yours alone to make. If you continue the pregnancy, you may learn a whole lot about yourself, your capacity for love, your relationship with your partner and the existence of a spirit world like I did.

I also felt it was important to tell this aspect of the story because every book I've seen on the topic of choosing life has come from a born-again or evangelical-type Christian perspective. As you can see, I am not coming from that perspective at all. I believe in a creator or creators and in energy and spirit living on in some form or another, perhaps in reincarnation, but that's as far as I've got it figured out.

People who seem so solid in their spiritual beliefs strike me as rather humorous. How can any of us *know*? I know the standard answer is faith. But faith is just believing in something without proof. I'm not trying to disparage religious folks, even though it may sound like I am. In a way I envy that certainty and comfort that they have about life, even if it's based not on proof but only faith.

We're told "God answers all prayers." Okay. But what if the answer is a loud "NO"? What's so special about God answering all prayers then? As you can see I'm far from having it all figured out.

I was in a deeply loving relationship with my partner when Quincy was conceived and I very much wanted her. I hoped and assumed, like most parents, that my baby would be born healthy. But I was ready to accept her, to fully love and help her just as she was. Dan had worked with disabled adults and children years before I met him when he lived in Alaska. I hoped that he would have the knowledge and strength to help me with whatever our little Quincy would present to us.

Although I was always pro choice politically, I never thought I'd choose abortion. I've always found it confusing that pro life proponents tend to be the same people who support foreign invasions and the right to bear arms. Many believe in capital punishment. I've never sat down with anyone from the pro life perspective and asked them how they reconcile what seems to me to be conflicting beliefs.

Whenever I want to figure out what is the right thing to do I think to myself, "What would Jesus do?" Well, he probably wouldn't advocate abortion, war, or capital punishment. But for those who have partaken in these acts, I'd imagine he'd forgive them or at least ask God to.

One day when I was about eight months pregnant with Tabitha, I drove to the mall in Carlsbad, California to pick up a few last-minute things I needed for the hospital. As I approached the entrance to the parking lot, there stood a couple of pro life protestors holding up a poster of a "partial birth abortion" that was literally about two-stories high. I called the police and the local newspaper.

"What if my child had been in the car and seen that?" I hollered. They didn't know I was only pregnant.

"I'm sorry, ma'am. It's free speech," I was told.

"Free speech, huh? Well, what if I were a pornographer and I decided to stand in a very busy intersection holding up a poster of two people having anal sex with each other. Is that free speech?"

"No. But, hey, I'm with you. I'd love to get rid of these guys. They're a nuisance and we get tons of calls about it," said the newspaper editor.

Chapter 9

Amnios and Ultrasounds

"Katie, I'll support you in whatever you want to do. You're the one who has to go through this. And it's not going to be easy any way you look at it," Dan said after Quincy's somersault protest.

A few weeks later we told this story to a prospective OB/GYN and he said that it's very unusual for a baby to move at all when a mother is in emotional distress.

"They usually bunch up and get very still in order to conserve energy, allowing the blood to flow to the mother's heart for the fight or flight response," he said.

"If I do carry her to term," I told Dan, "we're leaving space for the possibility of a miracle. And the doctors could be wrong, too, you never know. Ultrasounds aren't perfect."

I sat quietly for a few minutes.

"Dan, I'm changing my mind about the amnio," I declared.

"Are you sure you don't want to know for sure so we can be prepared?" Dan asked.

"If I get an amnio and it shows for certain that she's T18, then, in my mind, the chance of a miracle is almost non-existent. Plus they could accidentally hurt her or even induce labor."

I knew a woman who had lost her baby mid-pregnancy due to an amnio. Her doctor offered her an amniocentesis simply because she was over 35. I'm not a big fan of invasive interventions; I even question whether it's a good idea to get an ultrasound. Especially vaginal probe ultrasounds. I had one right before the second miscarriage that Dan and I had and, although it may be statistically unlikely that it was caused by the ultrasound probe, it sure felt like it.

It was a pregnancy clinic that advertised "Free Pregnancy Test and Ultrasound Screening" on the outside of the building. We didn't have health insurance at the time so it seemed that the only way to get an ultrasound was to pay for it out of pocket, which I couldn't afford, or to check out this place.

I walked into what appeared to be a low budget clinic and was instructed at the front desk to fill out some paperwork. The woman behind the counter informed me that there would be an extensive pre-screening interview before the ultrasound. After I filled out the paperwork, I was ushered into the pre-screening office.

"I see you are eight weeks pregnant. How are you feeling about being pregnant?" the screener asked.

"Fine, great," I responded, thinking this was an unusual interview. I was expecting questions about my health history.

"Wonderful. So are you married?" the woman asked.

"Yes," I said guardedly.

"Great. And are you planning to keep the baby?" she questioned.

"Yes, of course," I responded defensively, wondering if I had inadvertently wandered into a Planned Parenthood clinic. "I'm just here for your free ultrasound and pregnancy test. I need the pregnancy test confirmation so that I can apply for Medi-Cal for pregnancy since I don't have coverage at the moment."

"Ok, fine. Let me just ask you a few more questions first and then we can get started."

"Okay," I said, feeling like I had to play along to get what I came for.

"Have you ever had an abortion?"

"Yes."

"Oh, I see. And how do you feel about that today?"

"Why? What does that have to do with getting a pregnancy test and ultrasound?" I said edgily.

"Well, women who have had an abortion can regret it later, even years after getting one."

"Okay."

"Let me ask you… would you say you have a personal relationship with Jesus Christ our Lord?"

What had I walked into? There was no signage on the door that said anything about this being a religiously-affiliated clinic. It was a trap. But I had come this far and, like I said, I really needed this test so I answered her.

"I don't know. I guess so. But it's personal. I don't want to talk about it."

Seeing that she wasn't going to get anywhere with me, the screener led me back to the ultrasound room. I stripped down, put on the gown and lay on my back on the cold table. And waited, staring at the ceiling, thinking about what it means to have or not have a personal relationship with Jesus. Then my mind wandered to my comfort. I wondered why they always make it as cold and uncomfortable as possible in such offices. Once I had a female OB/GYN who gave out a pretty flowered, long cloth gown to wear and she put a modesty curtain in front of the door for added privacy. She decorated her exam rooms beautifully. A little touch that made a world of difference.

There was a knock at the door as it simultaneously flew open. In walked the ultrasound tech in plain clothes, no lab coat. I eyed her suspiciously. She didn't look like a medical ultrasound tech. Nevertheless, she began the procedure.

"Ouch, that hurts!" I exclaimed as she ground the vaginal probe around painfully.

"Sorry. I just want to see if I can get it at the right angle to pick up the heartbeat."

She couldn't.

"Maybe come back in a week or two and we'll try again," she said.

I had been down this road before. The moment no heartbeat was detected, I knew it was not a viable pregnancy. It was heartbreakingly disappointing. As I started to get dressed, I noticed I was spotting blood.

I left the clinic, got in my car and angrily slammed the door shut. I began sobbing. Of course I was crying about the impending miscarriage. But I also felt violated by the people at this clinic in every sense—spiritually, physically, and emotionally.

Chapter 10

Trisomy 18

The day after the birth center ultrasound of Quincy, Dan joined a Trisomy 18 Mommies Facebook group. Dan is always a take-action type of person.

"I can't go on there yet," I told him. "And I can't read about trisomy 18 either." I was in full-blown fear-based denial mode. This was very unusual for me. When I want to know something, I devour the topic, learning and researching every aspect of it. This topic I didn't want to know anything about. I didn't want to face the possibility that my baby was sick or worse.

"No problem. I'll do it for you and let you know only if I find out something important," Dan said gently.

Turns out this community is amazing. I was not much of a Facebook person up to this point. But this group offers true life support. They share medical information with each other from around the globe, information and solutions that are often passed on to their local doctors who didn't know how to treat their live T18 kids because, sadly, there's so few of them living.

One of the reasons there's so few trisomy 18 children living is that the vast majority of women who have babies diagnosed with trisomy 18 in an ultrasound choose to terminate the pregnancy.

This Facebook group of parents with children ranging in age from prenatal up to early adulthood, provides love, support, when necessary, condolences for each other. Many of them are single moms, having lost the support of their spouses during the tremendous stress and care that it takes to nurture and raise a child with trisomy 18. What the fathers who took off didn't know was how rewarding most of the mothers say it is to take care of these special children and the unconditional love they give to the people around them—most without ever speaking a word. They have a saying in the community: Trisomy 18 is a diagnosis NOT a prognosis. They are living evidence of this.

Women in their early teens and women at the other end of the reproductive spectrum are those most likely to have a baby with trisomy 18. Not that it's likely at all in either case. In the US alone, 1 out of every 2,500 pregnancies are diagnosed with T18; only 1 in 6,000 are live births.

"Kate, many of the women on the Trisomy 18 Mommies group say *not* to get an amnio," Dan informed me.

"Really?" I knew my reasons for not doing it but I had been oblivious to one of the potential outcomes of getting an amnio when trisomy 18 is suspected.

"Get this—if you do get an amniocentesis and it shows that Quincy has T18, then doctors have the *right to refuse to treat her.*"

"What?! No way. That can't be true!" I shouted incredulously. I was very emotional these days.

"The medical community thinks that most T18 kids won't live. If they do live, they're just a burden on society and their families and have no quality of life. And to try to give them medical care is unethical. Most doctors are taught in school that these children don't live past a year. Which just isn't true. There's a whole community of people here that prove that.

"This one woman in the community goes around the country speaking at medical ethics conferences. She said that the attitude toward T18 today is where the medical community was toward Down's syndrome (now known as Down syndrome or trisomy 31) in the 1950s: They're ignorant about it."

"That solidifies it. I'm *definitely* not getting the amnio," I declared.

And I didn't. I went on with my days, preparing as if I were going to have a healthy baby and healthy pregnancy. I did my prenatal exercise DVD daily. I took long walks in the hills. I ate well and took my prenatal vitamins. I made healthful fresh vegetable juices. I took fish oil.

And I went inward and pondered. What did this diagnosis mean, in real terms, for me and my family? And, most importantly, what, if anything, could I do to help effect a miracle? That may sound conceited to think that I, an insignificant human being in terms of the vast cosmos, could have any part in helping to bring about a miracle. After all, miracles, we're taught, are in the realm of God and the angels and saints. But I set aside that feeling of lack of worthiness and powerlessness. Deep inside of me I felt there was something I could do. I may not get the exact outcome I was looking for, but I could do something. I could effect some kind of change. At least, I felt I had to try.

As I told my friends and family about the ultrasound, I only described Quincy's physical situation. I didn't mention trisomy 18 or Downs. I was still in denial that she was likely T18. She could have Downs, which would be a far better scenario. Or she could be or become perfectly healthy.

Chapter 11
Proactive Sanity

Even under the best of circumstances, I typically don't have a restful mind. I found myself obsessed with the movie *The Secret* and the law of attraction. I had seen the law of attraction work in my life before. Not often but in some important instances. A few months before I met Danny I made a list of everything I wanted in a partner. It had something like 70 items on it. I was in my 30s, divorced, and had dated a good deal, so I knew exactly what type of person I would be compatible with. I also turned the list around and took a realistic look at it to see if I possessed a lot of the same characteristics I was looking for.

A month or so after meeting Dan I remembered the list. I pulled it out of my desk drawer and was shocked to see that he matched about 95% of the items on my wish list, even my very specific desires. It was really extraordinary.

But this time was different. I had to think about life on a quantum physics level now. Not that I even really fully understand what that means. As I understand it, our creator exists in the nanosphere of our cellular beings. Nothing was for certain with Quincy or any developing fetus, I thought. She was a growing organism, changing rapidly every day. My thoughts, my actions were sure to affect her. The question was how much?

Could what I was doing and thinking change her errant genetic map? If I knocked at God's door repeatedly, believing that a miracle had already happened, thanking Him or Her profusely, truly believing that a miracle could happen and that it actually had happened, would that miracle actually come into existence in the physical realm?

My daily mantra on my morning walks even before I had the negative ultrasound about Quincy was, "Thank you, God, for making my baby so beautiful, healthy, smart, strong, and kind." I'd say this aloud on my walks repeating it dozens of times. Why did I do this? I'd never done it before with my other two children. I was listening to Tony Robbins CDs at the time, which gave me the idea in order to help me reach my goals. But why did I do it with regard to my baby? Did I somehow know already that something was amiss?

As the pregnancy progressed and I felt more and more stress, getting out in nature and walking was a lifesaver. It helped to ground me, make me feel peaceful and safe. And it always has, no matter what is going on in my life. The sun rises and sets, birds and wildlife go about their business, everything fits together and is as it should be.

Whenever I pictured birthing at the hospital, I felt great anxiety. I just wanted to get in my truck and drive down to the beach and birth right there on the sand, with the sound of the ocean hypnotizing me. I knew this wasn't possible or at least not advisable at this point, but that visualization and being outdoors kept me temporarily calm and grounded.

I kept thinking there was more I could do. I am an action-oriented person—definitely to a fault. I could not just sit around and wonder each day if my baby was going to live. So I bought a rose quartz crystal and a regular quartz crystal and set them on top of my belly each night. They are both believed to have healing properties. Then I took my pregnancy belly speakers and plugged them into my computer, affixing the speakers to my lower belly. Every night I played classical music, Gregorian chants and Tibetan singing bowls for Quincy from YouTube. I had watched a Deepak Chopra documentary and he said that these types of music had the highest vibration and are the most healing.

She responded the most to the singing bowls, always moving around to the vibrations. I thought at the very least that I was giving her love and entertainment, parenting her then for however long she'd be with me. At the very most, I felt that I was helping to alter her physical vibration by sending her the highest energy sounds on the planet. I realized that she was not some far away visitor, to arrive on this planet on the day of her birth. She's here now; she's with us and a part of our family now.

One evening she got so into the Tibetan singing bowls that she kicked one of the crystals off my belly! How could she do that? How was that physically possible? She was so tiny at the time, probably not even 2 pounds. But she was mighty, in spirit and body.

Every morning I would lie very still in bed praying and waiting to feel some movement from her.

"Please, God, let her be alive today. Let me feel her kick."

As soon as I did feel her move, I would feel a rush of relief. She was safe for now; I can get up and on with my day. We made it another morning together.

Chapter 12

The Blessing Way

Shortly after we returned from the fateful ultrasound, I sent an email to some of my friends in Julian who had expressed a wish to have a blessing way for us. I had not been familiar with this ritual but learned that a blessing way is kind of like a baby shower but the focus is on supporting and nurturing the mother or family—presence not presents. Activities can include henna belly art, belly casting, washing the mother's feet and brushing her hair. For the less touchy-feely person like me, it could just include a special birthing necklace made for the mother. Each participant in the blessing way is asked to bring a special bead and a necklace is strung together, offering love and support of the mother during her birthing time.

In the email I informed everyone of what the possible reality could be for Quincy and that if we were going to do this blessing way, it should be sooner rather than later because she may not make it. It was so difficult to walk this fine line of complete hope and belief in having a healthy baby with the sadder thoughts of what the ultrasound showed.

They all rallied and planned the most amazing ceremony a couple of weeks later. I have never felt so loved and supported by friends before. And these were relatively new friends, too, people we had only known for a couple of years.

Every detail was given such careful love and consideration, from the delicious vegetarian fare to the solar-powered off-grid meeting room donated by Camp Stevens, to the beautiful fragrant bouquets of flowers scattered around the room. And no one felt the need to "talk about it." They just created a beautiful day for the four of us and sent us love.

Lydia, a city girl turned farmer hippie mom and midwifery student, brought her special family heirloom rocking chair to the event for me to sit on. Mati, who makes nature-inspired children's clothing out of recycled clothing and sells her wares on Etsy, made a crown of flowers for me to wear. Every person in the room said a few words of blessing to us as each person handed us a unique and specially selected natural stone bead.

There really was so much love in the room. Katalina, a nomadic and talented sculpture artist, presented us with a teak bowl filled with beach sand and beeswax candles. As the beads were presented to us, each person lit one of the candles. Dan, Tabitha, Willow, and I blew out the candles as if to wish Quincy a happy birthday. The blessings included kind words and well wishes about Quincy and our family. Cheyenne, a Native American mom who works for Cal Fire, said, "You think your story doesn't go beyond these walls, but it does. It goes to our friends and friends of friends and farther than you'll ever know. You are an inspiration to us."

The night before the gathering I had a dream that Quincy was born in a hospital with the help of a midwife. But instead of being Quincy, she looked like my friend Keri's son, Dakota, who was not quite a year old at the time. In my dream state, I was aware that the baby looked like a healthy and robust Dakota but at the same time I also knew he was really Quincy.

I told Keri about the dream at the blessing way and she said that was interesting because she, too, had a dream the night before about Quincy and Dakota. She said that the dream wasn't direct and linear like a story, but conveyed a sense that her Native American ancestors were speaking in energy waves through a very special tribal necklace that she owns. They were telling Dakota that he was supposed to take care of Quincy or guide her in some way. She said it felt to her that the two souls were linked in some way. The dream was surrounded with warmth and a feeling of protection. As we would find out later, Quincy and Dakota would share the same birthday, one year apart.

Dan made a somewhat tearful speech. As he concluded and reached over to touch the side of my belly, Quincy woke up and kicked in the exact spot before he touched it. Again, she was so aware of her surroundings. It was as if she existed simultaneously inside and outside of me, able to see, feel and hear everything around me. It was quite an unusual experience. Repeatedly she would respond to outside comments and stimuli.

One day our fairy spirit Willow was dancing around the kitchen with her magic wand.

"Willow," I asked, "why don't you give Quincy a magic healing spell with your wand?"

We had told the girls from the start what was going on with Quincy, in what we thought were age-appropriate terms they could understand. We also told them that we were hoping and believing a miracle would happen. I thought this might be a mistake, getting their hopes up about having a healthy baby sister, or any baby sister. But I believe children are powerful in their wishes and beliefs. I wanted their power behind us.

Willow danced over to me and waved her little wand over my tummy very close to it but without touching. Quincy, who had been asleep or at least very quiet the moment before, kicked *in the exact spot* beneath Willow's hovering "magic" wand.

After the excitement of the blessing way was over, I continued to do my daily affirmation mantras, crystals, exercises, and songs for Quincy. We all felt buoyed by the love and attention our friends gave us. And it made me feel more hopeful than ever in the possibility of a healing miracle for Quincy.

Chapter 13

Prayer in Numbers

While I had been doing many things to try to help nurture and heal Quincy, I couldn't help but think there must be more I could be doing. Then I remembered something I had read once about an experiment done with prayer. I wish I could remember the details of it, but the gist of it was that if enough people pray for the same outcome, that outcome sometimes can and has happened.

So I asked the one person I knew who knows a lot of people who like to pray—my aunt Mary Jo. She had been a nomadic Catholic nun for over 30 years, traveling with various circuses through small towns in the US. She knew scores of people from living on the road for so many years. And she had been asked innumerable times to pray for her friends around the world. Maybe she could ask them to pray for her niece and her baby, I thought.

"I'd be honored to. Give me a few days to put together an email and send it out. I'll let you know what happens," she said.

Her friends responded in droves. Every day she'd forward me emails from her friends who said they would be happy to pray for Quincy and our family. And not only were her friends praying, but they were asking their friends and parishes to pray for us as well. I felt so very humble and appreciative of the support of these people I had never met.

Many years ago, well before having children, I tried hallucinogenic mushrooms just to see what it would be like. I wouldn't do it again and I don't recommend using substances that take you out of yourself. Although some cultures have used it as a tool to achieve a glimpse of enlightenment, I think there are better and safer ways to reach the same goal. Namely, through meditation, clean living, yoga, and the like.

Anyway, at the time that I tried it, enlightenment wasn't the goal. My purpose was fueled by curiosity, entertainment, and a desire for adventure. Mostly I just giggled a lot when "shrooming" and watched *Fantasia* with some friends. But at the end of the movie, I felt something I hadn't expected. I felt a complete oneness with everyone in my community and somewhat beyond that. I could literally feel that we were all connected. I could feel them sitting in their living rooms, laughing, sharing, watching TV, living life. This was before I'd even given much thought to a higher consciousness.

I now know that we are all connected and part of one spirit because I felt it. I could see it with my mind's eye—sort of a back-of-the-mind non-visual yet vague imagery and knowingness of an intimate connection between human beings and within one spirit. It's very hard for me to describe.

While carrying Quincy, I got to thinking about that higher consciousness. If Mary Jo and her friends and our friends would pray for Quincy and possibly help to effect a miracle, wouldn't even more people praying possibly make a bigger difference, increasing the odds of success? At some level, I knew it was ridiculous to try to quantify the spirit world in this manner. But a part of me—the hopeful, desperate, intuitive and questioning part—thought it was a possibility and definitely worth a try.

One afternoon I came up with the idea to purchase an email mailing list as a way to reach as many people as possible. I purchased a list for about 100,000 churches in the US. I would have obtained a list of temples and synagogues, too, but this list was the largest and most affordable. I bought it from listsyoucanafford.com. I was having some difficulty using their payment system so it was taking longer than I wanted to receive the list. Hoping to expedite the process, I told the owner what I wanted to use it for, conveying to him that time was of the essence. He responded quickly and threw in another 200,000 church emails for free!

And every night that I had the energy, I would send out up to 1,000 emails to churches asking them to put us on their prayer list. I know this probably sounds hypocritical of me, given what I've said about my own religious practices. Even though I don't attend any religious institution and I don't take my children to one, this was the only way I knew to reach a lot of people who would actually follow through on the prayers.

And they did. Every day I would get dozens of emails from churches saying they would pray for us and they believed that she was already healed. We boldly asked them to pray in a certain way for us. I believed that prayers of pity wouldn't work. It would just feed more negative energy into her developing being. It had to be a positive prayer, as if a miracle had already occurred and she had already been healed. Here is the email we sent:

Hello,

We'd like to request that your congregation pray for our third daughter, Quincy Rose Marsh. I am 30 weeks pregnant with her. We live in a small mountain community in San Diego County, CA. We have had several ultrasounds that show she has heart trouble, a **cleft lip**, and other markers for trisomy 18. Please help us pray for a miracle of complete healing for her.

Jesus said in Mark 11:24, "I tell you then, whatever you ask for in prayer, believe that you *have* received it and it *will* be yours." So we ask that you offer an affirmative prayer such as this: "Thank you, God, for healing Quincy Rose Marsh and making her so beautiful, healthy, smart, strong and kind." We believe that miracles are possible and that in this case it has already happened.

Thank you so much for your time, support and for allowing us to frame the wording of your prayer in the affirmative present tense. If you let us know that you plan to pray for her, we will keep in touch and let you know how she is doing later this year.

Best Regards,
Katie, Dan, Tabitha, Willow & Quincy Marsh

Chapter 14

Buddha in the Storm

At the same time I was "doing" all of this, I pondered the Buddhist concept of receptivity, of being detached from any outcome. Of course, this was pretty much the exact opposite philosophy of what I was doing. But I believe there is some truth to the Buddhist approach. If you can just have an open heart and love everyone and be still and present in your current circumstances, free from want and attachment to outcomes, by definition you will be free from pain. And you may even get the outcome you no longer care one way or another about getting. You can't feel pain when you don't have attachment to anything. But how can one do that when it relates to the ones we love? This sounds difficult enough for a celibate Buddhist monk but for a person with a family, wouldn't it be impossible?

I became friends with a Buddhist monk in Thailand a couple of years before I met Dan. I was working as a freelance court reporter in the Washington, DC area and hating my life. No satisfying romantic relationships, no meaningful work. My sister, Kara, went to New Zealand to meet up with a friend and go backpacking. Every week Kara would send out amazing emails of her adventures. I so missed hanging out with her.

One day I went into a bookstore in Alexandria, VA, with my boyfriend at the time and found a great book of stories about women who have traveled the world, either alone or with friends. But it was only about women and their adventures. I bought and devoured it in a couple of days. Between Kara's adventurous emails and this incredible book, I was very inspired. This is what I wanted to do. It was time to see the world. And if I was very lucky, maybe I'd fall in love along the way. I told my boyfriend.

"I'm going to join my sister and backpack for a while," I avowed.

"For how long?" he asked, probably assuming I'd do the usual two-week vacation type thing.

"I don't know… six months, a year, something like that."

"Why would I let you do that?" he asked.

"Why would you *let* me do that?" I laughed.

The look on his face showed that he realized how silly his words were. We cared for each other but we both knew the relationship wasn't going anywhere. And when he made that statement, I knew for sure that I wasn't leaving anything special behind. He was not a bad guy at all; I know his controlling statement was just coming from a place of fear over the impending loss of our relationship and his own looming loneliness.

In all fairness to him, I tended to do whatever I pleased back then and not consider the feelings of the people around me. I've always been on the move and I know that many people don't understand or easily accept this. They just feel loss while I'm on to the next adventure. I do feel loss, too, but it's not as poignant for the one doing the moving as it is for the one who stays behind with reminders of special times everywhere around them.

I emailed Kara and told her of my plans to join her. In retrospect, I should have asked her if I could join her. She was on a journey of her own and I think she wanted to be a free spirit, able to travel when and where she desired without hindrance.

At the time, tourists from the US could only stay in New Zealand for a certain number of months, after which they would have to leave and go somewhere, anywhere, for a little while before returning to the country. So many backpackers would go to Australia, Thailand or other Southeast Asian countries, and spend some time traveling there before returning. Besides being a culturally enriching experience, traveling through Southeast Asia was just a short flight away and at the time very affordable for Western travelers.

It didn't take me long to sell most of my things. After a few yard sales, I was down to just the essentials and the rest I stored at my grandmother's place. I was to join Kara in Thailand first. But I really had no idea how or what to pack as I had never been backpacking before. I went to an outdoor superstore to stock up on some overpriced "essentials." I called her from the store.

"Hey, Kara, do you think I'll need a snake bite kit?" I asked.

"What? No. We're staying in bungalows."

"What about this water purifying kit?"

"We'll buy bottled water. Get a backpack, a couple changes of clothes, and I'll see you here."

I hung up with her a little doubtful. How could that be all I'd need? I had needed a lot more things than that just to survive living in one place. I decided to purchase the snake bite kit just in case. Little did either of us know when we spoke that our travels would take us to very different places. As it turns out, I actually could have used that water purification kit.

I landed in Bangkok very weary after traveling for 22 hours by myself in several different airplanes. I was wearing a tank top and my sporty new khaki pants, the kind that unzip at the knee so they can convert into long shorts. As I waited for my backpack on the carousel, I scanned the terminal, wondering where Kara was. We had planned to meet right there.

My backpack finally appeared on the conveyor. I hoisted it up onto my shoulders and immediately lost my balance, almost falling completely supine before quickly chucking it off one shoulder. It was too heavy—way too heavy. How had I not noticed this before I left? And where was Kara? I started to feel very anxious. What had I done? Maybe this traveling idea wasn't such a good one. I felt overwhelmed. I knew no one here but my sister, assuming I could find her. So far this country looked more foreign to me than any place I'd ever been before. I couldn't even read any of the signs in the airport.

I searched out a cart and although I must have looked pretty foolish putting my backpack on it, I figured that I had no choice until I got to a hotel and had a chance to unload some of my goodies.

Finally I saw Kara cruising into the airport, all tan with long shorts, flip flops, cute braided pigtails with an iPod cord coming out of her ears. That was something I forgot to pack, I thought.

Our adventures together are enough material for another book. We spent a lot of time traveling by train and bus to the usual backpacker destinations, staying in small thatched bungalows at night. Since we were on different time stays on our visas, Kara had to leave Thailand to renew her visa before I had to leave. After about a month and a half or two of traveling together, she departed for Australia and I decided to continue traveling by myself in Thailand. I had no set itinerary and I liked it that way.

"I'm going to miss you," I told her.

"Me, too. But we'll catch up again. I've got a lead on a job working on a farm outside of Sydney. When your visa runs out, come join me over there."

"Sounds good. Be careful."

Most of the travelers we met were from Canada, Israel, Australia, and Germany. We only met a few people from the US. It's just not in our cultural fabric to aimlessly travel, I suppose. We go to school, get a job, take a two-week vacation maybe, usually to someplace safe within the US or outlying islands or possibly venture to Europe. Not so much east of there unless you're from a foreign country and have family there. It's way more common for young people from other countries to take some time off to travel before going to university or joining the military.

It was a wonderful experience that I would highly recommend. But I think it's better to always travel with a friend and tell loved ones back home where you are going at all times.

The day after Kara departed for Sydney, I took a stroll along the Chao Phraya River in Bangkok, looking for the closest ferry stop. I had all day to myself to do whatever I wanted. The sky was clear and although the air was humid, it seemed less polluted than usual. Fewer locals were wearing respirators. As I walked down the river, a young monk, who looked to be about my age, dressed in orange robes with a shaved head was walking in the opposite direction. We smiled at each other then we both spontaneously stopped to chat.

"Hello! Do you speak English?" he asked.

"Yes, I do."

"Are you American?" he inquired.

"Yes," I said, slightly surprised wondering what it was about me that made him guess that.

"My name is Boontom [pronounced Bun Tom]."

"Katie. Nice to meet you."

I tried to shake his hand but he recoiled. I found out later that Buddhist monks are not allowed to touch a woman, even accidentally. If they do, they have to go through a whole-day purification ritual. A woman can't even hand a monk a piece of paper. You have to set it down on something first, and then the monk can pick it up. My guess is that it has to do with the transfer of tempting sexual energy, but I don't know the reason for sure.

"I would like to practice speaking English with you, okay?"

"Sure, I'd like that."

I reversed my course and joined him for a walk up the river, chatting with him about my travels. He told me that he was 35, same age as me, and that he had been a monk since he was 15. He taught English and art at the wat, which is a Buddhist monastery temple and school.

"Would you like to come with me to visit my wat?"

I had no set plans for the day. "Right now?" He nodded. "Sure, why not?"

We took the ferry across the river and entered the small but ornate temple. Young men dressed in orange robes were everywhere, shyly looking at me. Boontom bought me a Coke and introduced me around. We didn't stay very long, for some reason, and returned to the ferry after about 15 minutes.

"I invite many English-speaking people to come to my wat but you are the first person to say yes."

I told him that I would be leaving soon for Australia to renew my visa, but I planned to return to Thailand in three months when my visa there expired. We exchanged addresses and to my amazement we kept in touch by mail. Boomtom always drew me these beautiful pen drawings of scenes from his homeland along with the letters which he folded into origami-like shapes.

"When you return to Thailand, I will not be a monk any longer and we can travel together to visit my family, if you'd like," he wrote.

Worried that this was tantamount to a priest leaving the priesthood, I discouraged him from making this decision. "It is not a problem. And it is the only way for me to travel with you. I am not allowed to travel alone with you as a monk," he wrote.

Since Boontom's English was not very good, I couldn't get a full explanation from him about this. So I bought and read a book written by an Englishman who had become a Buddhist monk in Thailand. In the book he explains that almost all Thai Buddhists become monks for a short period when they come of age in order to make merit for their ancestors in the afterlife. Many stay on as monks, especially young men from poor areas, because it is a way to be fed, clothed, and educated.

And as a monk, you are at the highest level of status in society. Even the prime minister bows to the monks. Boontom later told me that leaving the monkhood meant a slight demotion in status when one returned, but one could leave and return without too much fuss.

Three months later I returned to Thailand, as promised, and met Boontom at a bus station. He looked so different in his blue jeans, hat, and backpack. I was surprised that someone who had lived most of his life in orange robes could look so naturally stylish.

We had about four hours to kill before the bus arrived so we had plenty of time to talk. He told me about *binderbaht*, where monks walk around town at about 4 a.m. with a big bowl and Buddhist families fill their bowls with specially-prepared food, not just leftovers from the night before. The monks take the food back to the temple and eat a large meal once a day, sometimes twice. In between studies, meals, and binderbaht, they spend hours in meditation.

I thought about how different my new friend's life had been from mine to date.

"What have you not tried, Boontom, that you would like to try now that you have this temporary freedom?"

He thought about it for a moment. "I've never drank alcohol. And…" he said shyly, "I've never kissed."

I leaned over and gave him a light kiss on the lips. He smiled the kind of smile you just can't help but stare at. Boontom's teeth were perfectly straight and white. I'm sure he never had orthodonture work. Then I remembered a book I read about people who live close to the land. They usually have perfect teeth. It's when you introduce a Western diet to a mother that it can affect the palate and teeth of the babies in the next generation.

"Check one off the list! Now let's go get you a beer. Take it slowly. I think one beer should make you quite happy."

He followed me like a puppy to the bus terminal 7-Eleven. There are 7-Elevens all over Bangkok but most of what they carry is very unfamiliar to most Westerners: dried fish snacks, cultured yogurt drinks, and various local brands of products.

We slept on most of the long bus ride to northern Thailand. The sunrise warmed my face and woke me about an hour from our destination. As we approached his rural hometown, I became a bit anxious. How well did I know Boontom? We had corresponded quite a bit but we weren't close friends yet. But he must be a good man, I rationalized. He had been a monk for 20 years.

Suddenly it occurred to me that I didn't exactly know where I was going. If you've never traveled any length of time as a backpacker, this behavior must seem foolhardy and bizarre. But to travelers, it's all part of the adventure. I'm not defending it and saying it was smart of me in any way. But in my zest for experiencing something unique, I realized that I hadn't fully thought this through.

"Boontom," I asked a little nervously, trying to gather more information, "when was the last time you saw your family?"

He smiled. "About 20 years ago."

"Twenty years ago?! They must be so excited that you're coming!"

"I haven't told them yet," he smiled impishly.

"Boontom!" I scolded, "What will they think when you come traipsing in after all these years—and with me?"

He just laughed. "Don't worry, no problem."

We disembarked at the bus stop and then walked down a muddy road. The air was thick and humid and the morning sun was already starting to burn my fair skin. In the distance, I could see a few houses alongside the road. It didn't really look like a town, as there were no shops, only some makeshift houses on either side of a muddy dirt road lined up next to each other.

As we approached, people gathered barefoot in the road. All the people were barefoot and wearing American-brand clothing but with mismatched colors and patterns. They stared incredulously at me and then at Boontom. Soon they recognized him and rushed forward to greet us, surrounding, and hugging him. They were speaking very quickly in a language I didn't understand, a unique regional dialect that was a combination of Lao and Thai. No one spoke English so Boontom translated—not what was actually said but his version of a summary.

"They must be so excited to see you after all of these years," I said, stating what I thought to be the obvious.

"They're more excited to see you."

"What? Why?"

"Because they've never seen a Westerner before. They have never seen anyone with white skin."

I was stupefied. How was this possible in today's world of planes, trains and automobiles (and one of my favorite movies, too)? Boontom was quite the mischievous monk bringing me here unannounced to his village. But he was having fun surprising his family, so I went along with it.

After the warm greetings, he took me over to his grandmother's house to surprise her next. She was squatting on the floor in front of a wood-burning stove plucking a chicken. She spotted us walking in and leapt up to her feet, still holding the chicken by the neck as she rushed forward to give Boontom a hug. She was overcome with happiness seeing her grandson after 20 years. She spoke very excitedly while looking at him, then at me, then back to him again.

"What is she saying?" I asked, while smiling at her self-consciously.

"She is saying, 'You two will make the most beautiful porcelain white babies.'"

I froze. I had never promised Boontom anything. Did he have the wrong impression or was this just the hope of a grandmother who desperately wanted great grandbabies? In Thailand, white skin is revered. It is a sign of status. Women working in the rice paddies have tanned brown skin; women working in offices or wealthy women who don't have to work stay indoors or walk outside with umbrellas and have much paler skin. Many Thai women also use special bleaching creams to make their skin whiter.

After everyone settled down, I guess there was some talk about going for a hike. So a couple dozen members of his family gathered and led us on a long stroll through the off-road countryside. Besides having pale white skin, I was taller than everyone in the village by at least a head. We began our journey by gingerly walking on a rickety rope bridge that was strung across a slow-moving stream. I was mostly watching my feet, but I couldn't help but notice a group of untethered bulls in a field to my right. Each one had a different sized cowbell roped around its neck. As they grazed on the lush green grass, each bell made a unique and beautiful tinkling sound. But when they spotted me in the middle of the line of people crossing the bridge, every single one of the bulls stopped eating and looked up. It must really be true, I thought, that I am the first tall, pale Westerner to ever visit. I'm even startling the bulls!

The children kept quite a distance from me but their curiosity was obvious as they peeked out from behind the adults to smile at me. I noticed that it was almost impossible to tell which child belonged to which parent. All of the adults seemed to be taking care of each of the children at one point or another. So this is where the concept of "it takes a village to raise a child" must come from. Or, at least, it was a great example of it.

We stopped several times along our hike and everyone took turns taking group photos of each other. Boontom was quite into photography and promised to send me copies. After a few hours, all of us seemed to become simultaneously tired and hungry, the high heat and humidity sapping everyone's energy. We stopped at a lean-to along the path just as it began to rain. But this didn't stop them; everyone went to work, automatically knowing which job to do. Someone caught a fish in the stream, another gathered fruit, someone else chopped and prepped—everyone had a job in preparing the meal and gathering whatever they could find growing around us to eat.

As the special guest my job was to hang out. (I tried offering my help, but it was refused.) When they were finished preparations, I found it to be one of the most delicious Thai meals I'd ever eaten. In particular there was this one lemony-tasting fish and rice dish. When I looked down at it to try to discover what the ingredients were so that I could replicate it one day, I was appalled to discover that it was covered in *dead red ants*.

"Boontom! What's wrong with this fish dish? Why is it covered in ants?"

"Don't worry," he laughed. "When we can't find lemon, we use the ants. They taste like lemon. Very good for you."
"But how did you kill them all?"

"Drowned."

It was so tasty but I just couldn't bring myself to take another bite. I surreptitiously looked around at my hosts making sure no one was noticing me pile my plate with other food while scattering my ant-covered fish dish around my plate like a child trying to hide uneaten food from her parents.

That evening back in town, Boontom's grandmother graciously gave us the largest room in the house to sleep in, displacing his oldest male cousin. The room was for us to sleep in together. I felt like it was a bridal suite and she was hoping we'd make some of those porcelain white babies for her that evening. When we were in the room alone together, Boontom expressed his feelings for me.

"I love you, Katie. I will go anywhere with you or we can be here together. You can teach English in our village."

"Boontom, I love you like a friend. I can't live here with you."

It was tempting to stay and teach English here—what an amazing experience it would be for me and for them. I didn't need a Starbucks to be happy but I was reaching my comfort threshold, as the area lacked most modern amenities such as toilet paper and clean water. But Boontom was so sweet and sincere in his profession of love for me that it did give me pause. He was a very nice and good man and we did have fun together. But our backgrounds were so different. And I knew I didn't have a heart-felt love for him. It made me question myself. What was wrong with me? Why was I in my mid-30s and unable to fall in love with anyone? It wasn't for lack of opportunities or trying. I had even been married before and that hadn't worked out. Was I just afraid to be close to anyone?

I was having a lot of physical issues since visiting this small village somewhere in northern Thailand. The sticky rice we were eating had me backed up for four days. The rice was so sticky you could literally roll a ball of it up in your palm and almost play ping-pong with it. Not only that but period cramps were affecting me and there was no place to put my tampons because there were no trash piles here. These issues and an all-encompassing humidity made me feel just disgusting.

And the whole pushing us to have babies scenario was really starting to freak me out. I panicked. I realized I was completely dependent on Boontom's kindness to get me out of here as I had no idea where I was. What if they kept me here and made me become an English-teaching porcelain baby-making slave? Okay, so it was unlikely but you never know.

"Boontom, I want to go back to Bangkok in the morning," I declared nicely but firmly.

He looked sad for a long moment. "Okay. We will take the bus in the morning."

Detachment. That's the Buddhist way. He wanted to be with me because I was the first woman he'd ever kissed and because he had a fascination with all things American. Most other men would have tried persuasion, but not my dear monk friend. He was still a monk at his core and he detached his feelings, his wants, in order to make me comfortable and happy.

Chapter 15
Psychic Moments and Little G

In keeping with all the doing and not detaching during my pregnancy with Quincy, I spent time doing healing visualizations for her. I would picture a healing pinkish white light coming down from the heavens towards the earth, down to California, zeroing in on Julian and then through the roof of our house and into the crown of my head, down my spine and into my womb, enveloping her with healing energy. I'd picture her every day in perfect health and comfort inside of me surrounded by this pinkish white light.

I first learned to do healing techniques and clairvoyant readings a couple of Christmases earlier. Dan gave me the book *Are You Psychic?* I laughed when I opened it.

"What's so funny?" he asked.

"You'll see."

He reached into his stocking and pulled out a book from me called *You Are Psychic*, by Debra Lynne Katz. We both had a good chuckle over it. I started to read the book he gave me first but it didn't really resonate with me. So I put it down and devoured his instead. It was amazing. Debra posits that every one of us has psychic ability, but some of us need to learn a few visualization exercises in order to tap into it. The book teaches a lengthy creative visualization exercise in order to get you in the right space to perform a clairvoyant reading. Once you're there, you just sit back and wait for images to come to you in your mind's eye. The tricky part is interpreting the images correctly. The images are often accurate psychic impressions but understanding what they mean can be difficult. The book also teaches how to conduct psychic healings through visualization work.

I've practiced these techniques fairly regularly for the past three years. I'm not a big believer in the psychic healing part since I haven't seen it work yet. But I have had quite a few uncanny experiences with psychic readings. I'm still trying to learn what many of the images mean. But I can always tell it's a message from the spirit world when the image is either something I'm unfamiliar with or in cartoon form. When it's a regular image of something that I would or could normally conjure up myself, then I'm less certain of its accuracy.

Sometimes, very rarely, the psychic intuition comes to me naturally, without having to prepare myself with these visualization techniques. For example, a month ago I was zoning out and painting my kitchen in our new house in Maine. The cabinets were an ugly brown, making the kitchen look even smaller than it is. I was brightening them up with some sunshine yellow paint when I remembered a day that I took my grandma to her bank to make a deposit. It was a day when we were running several errands—there was nothing special about it. My grandmother and I were very close and she passed away over five years ago. I definitely miss her but I don't think about her every day any longer and I certainly don't think about her estate, which had been settled and closed a few years ago. As I received this image, I suddenly had the overwhelming feeling that she had left some of her money in that bank.

I put the paint brush down and went to my computer. How could I find this out? I couldn't very well call the bank and ask them if my deceased grandmother's money was still there, could I? I poked around on the Internet and after a while found a site called missingmoney.com. Sure enough, there were three accounts in my grandmother's bank linked to her name and former address that had reverted to the comptroller of the State of Maryland because nobody in our family knew about their existence.

I called the comptroller. "Hi, I have three claim numbers here linked to some accounts that my grandmother owned. She passed away five years ago."

"I'm sorry for your loss. What is her Social Security number?"

"No idea."

"Call your nearest Social Security office. They'll tell you what you need to do to get that information."

So I called the nearest office, which is an hour and a half from where we live in northernmost Maine. It turns out it's not so clear cut on how to get someone else's Social Security number.

"Just come into the office and bring something with you to prove your relationship to your grandmother."

"How can I do that? What should I bring?" I asked.

"I don't know."

I pondered it for a day or two. What could I bring with me that would prove that my grandmother was my grandmother? Then I remembered a book I had written for her called *The Birth of Dying: Explore End-of-Life Issues with Your Terminally Ill or Elderly Loved One*. There are no answers in this book, only questions and you provide the answers that are right for you.

It's a workbook that addresses most of the concerns and questions we all have about aging and dying. It is designed to be worked through by two people together: daughter to parent, husband to wife, friend to friend, loved one to loved one. The goal of the book is to facilitate a settling of financial and legal affairs, making funeral arrangements, sharing fears and other feelings, and creating a memoir for loved ones.

I had written it for her when she was living in an assisted living home in Maryland due to her declining health. My aunt Mary Jo had been living there with her in the home and caring for her. She wanted a way to communicate with her mother about end-of-life issues and a way to help her finish her memoir. So I wrote and self-published the workbook, and Dan and his sister Tahnee helped me rush it to press one weekend as Little G's health was rapidly declining. I FedExed it overnight to her, hoping she would get it in time, even though I knew she was too ill at that point to make much use of it. The book arrived a half hour after she passed away.

Before Dan and I knew of her passing, we were playing with Tabitha on our bed early that morning. The shades were drawn and it was barely light enough to see in the room. Tabitha was about 11 months old at the time. She sat up on top of me and looked over to the corner of the room, smiling and waving.

"What do you see, Tabitha?" Dan asked. There was nothing in the corner of the room, not even a plant or a picture.

"Who are you waving at?" I asked.

But she wasn't very verbal yet so all she could do was continue waving and smiling. A few hours later I got a call from Mary Jo informing us of my grandmother's death.

During the entire month after her death, the smoke detector kept sounding off. We must have pulled the battery out and replaced it a dozen times. As new parents, Dan and I made the mistake of buying Tabitha every fun, noisy toy we could find, not realizing how annoying these toys can be. During this month, every toy that could make noise in our house did, intermittently *without being touched or turned on*. We felt it was my grandmother's presence in our house as she transitioned from this world into the next.

In *The Birth of Dying*, I mention my grandmother by name in the acknowledgement section. I thought maybe this could serve as proof of our relationship. We tend to believe what we see in print and there was no reason to think I'd write an entire book just to try to get her Social Security number from the Social Security Administration. It would be soft proof at best, but it might work.

Suddenly I got the chills as I remembered that a couple of days earlier at the same exact spot in our kitchen where I had been painting and envisioned my grandmother going to the bank, I had an image of this book. It was a fleeting thought about a day Dan and I took it to a retirement community to propose using it in a workshop for the residents. It was just a random thought; I didn't dwell on it at the time. But days later it seemed to me to be related to the first idea of missing money. I interpreted it as another message, perhaps from my grandmother, of how to prove my relationship to her. Since then we half-jokingly dubbed that part of the house "The Psychic Portal."

Tabitha was at school and Willow was released early as she was just in pre-K. I packed her up in the truck and we drove together an hour and a half to the nearest Social Security office. We walked in and I presented the book to the clerk.

"I need my grandmother's Social Security number," I said, handing the woman my ID and pointing out that my middle name is the same as my grandmother's last name. She looked at me as if she were going to say "we need more than that." I cut her off at the pass.

"And I wrote this book for her," I said, sliding *The Birth of Dying* under her window. I asked her to turn to the acknowledgement page. The clerk looked at it unflinchingly.

"One moment, please. I need to check with my supervisor." She returned five minutes later and furtively looked around while quickly scribbling down my grandmother's SSN on a piece of paper. She slid it to me under the glass with a look that told me to take it and run.

"Here you go," she said hurriedly.

Five minutes later from my truck I called the comptroller. There was almost $30,000 in the accounts.

Chapter 16

Other People's Miracles

I continued my birth preparations for Quincy's arrival. As many pregnant women do, I was working on my 18-year to-do list, trying to complete every project possible before I had no free time ever again. I cleaned, I organized and I bought stuff. In fact, we purchased everything we could possibly need for her from Target. Since we had moved so often and weren't originally planning to have a third child, we had given away or sold most of the baby supplies we had.

As we shopped online, a part of me felt so joyful and proactive about such a tangible display of hopefulness, not just to the outside world but to myself. Surely if I had all of these goodies for her—baby clothes, washtub, swing—she would be here to use them. I kept ignoring the practical and sad little voice in my head that said the risk wasn't so great in buying these things; you could always return her stuff if she doesn't make it.

It was a terrible feeling to simultaneously experience the joy, excitement, and expectation of a new baby tempered with the looming fear and possible reality that she may not live. But she felt so good, so alive inside of me, moving around in my womb like my other girls had.

And my belly was growing so big. Too big, actually. Because Quincy's esophagus was not connected to her stomach, she wasn't able to swallow the amniotic fluid. I didn't even know babies did this or why it was important before. But because she wasn't swallowing it, it was creating excess fluid in my womb.

"It's a condition called polyhydramnios," Dr. Z said. "It could get to be too much for you at the end of the pregnancy. If it becomes difficult to breathe, we can drain some of the excess fluid off."

Difficult to breathe? What was I in for? A suffocating end to my pregnancy—and possibly to my life—with a baby who may or may not live? This pregnancy was becoming very overwhelming and frightening. And each visit with a doctor would bring more disturbing news. I found myself developing a major fear of going to all doctors' appointments, even ones not related to my pregnancy.

With each new bit of bad news for me and/or Quincy, I found myself feeling temporarily detached from her, and anxious about my own health. Of course, concerns about myself and not my baby would inevitably bring on a wave of guilt about what a selfish mother I must be. But once the feelings of guilt subsided, I'd boomerang to the other end of the spectrum of emotions.

I would find myself feeling absolutely justified in my concerns for myself and at the same time quite indignant about the medical community's assumption that I was here just to incubate a baby. The assumption seemed to be that since I eschewed the idea of having an abortion, I would do whatever it took to bring my baby into the world, even at my own peril. It was never put in those exact words to me, but all discussions and assumptions that I faced from every doctor and other caregivers seemed to be based on that tacit premise.

As many women have experienced during pregnancy, people tend to make comments about your size. "Oh, you're so small!" Or "You're all belly!" Nothing is usually said if you blimp up, except, in my experience, a midwife once when I was carrying Tabitha and I gained 65 pounds.

"What have you been doing, sitting around and eating junk food all day?" she said, without looking up from her chart.

I was furious, and extremely embarrassed.

"Look at me!" I demanded. "Do I look obese to you?"

She looked up from her paperwork and studied me for a moment.

"Well, no," she conceded.

I had been very underweight before I became pregnant with Tabitha. Even though I walked five to six miles on the beach almost every day of my pregnancy, I couldn't help but be ravenously hungry and eat everything I could find. I ate four solid meals a day plus snacks.

During this pregnancy, my body remained skinny but my belly grew bigger until it started to look like I was carrying twins.

I kept working on all the things I was doing to help my little Quincy, which also helped me to maintain my sanity. If I could keep busy with activities that may help her, then I wouldn't have to focus on how scared I was. Scared for her, scared for me. Scared of the effect she could have on our family, whether she lived or died.

If she was born trisomy 18 and had special needs, how much time and attention would that take away from our other two girls? It would for certain affect the course of their lives and not necessarily in a positive way. They would not have parents who had the time and energy to do all that good parents do.

They would not have the parents they had now who took them to ballet classes and on hikes and to soccer games; who had the time and energy to plan great birthday parties. The parents who played with them and did crafts and cooking projects with them. Those parents are already stretched thin with the everyday struggles with health and money and the lack of a local extended family support structure. With an extremely health-challenged child, those parents would be gone.

I devoted considerable time to the emails. Besides feeling Quincy move around in response to the Tibetan singing bowls, I found the emails extremely rewarding. Every day I would find myself crying because of the warmth and love given to my family by strangers. People who never met us earnestly cared and prayed for her and for our family, and all of Mary Jo's friends who were more than happy to repay the favor for all of her prayers for them over the years. And then there was the occasional inspiring miracle story someone would send me, something that I would cling to every day for hope. Here's one of the miracle emails:

"Dear Marsh Family,
I am an administrative assistant for the Sisters here at the monastery and will be sure to give them your prayer request for baby Quincy Rose. (That is my middle name, too.) I will also ask the people at my church to pray for her as we have some wonderful prayer warriors there.

"When I was two months pregnant with our daughter K_____, I went to the doctor for a routine ultrasound and could see the alarm on the technician's face. I asked her what was wrong, and instead of answering me, she went to get the doctor. He did another ultrasound himself, and they told me that there was no heartbeat, no movement… nothing. I was devastated. He said he could give me something to help my body abort the dead fetus, or I could wait and let it happen naturally. I chose to wait.

"A few days later, we were having a revival at our church and while the evangelist was preaching, he walked down the aisle, held out his hand and asked me [to] step out. He said the Lord had told him that I needed a mighty miracle, and I was going to receive it. I had told nobody in the church about my situation, so there is no way in the world he could have known this on his own. He put his hands on my stomach and began to pray for me, as did the church people.

"A week later I asked the doctor for another ultrasound. He thought it was pointless, but in I went, and there on the screen was my K_____ squirming around… strong heartbeat. It almost looked like she was waving at us to let everyone know she was there and well!!! She turned 9 in January and is 'beautiful, healthy, smart, strong and kind.' People at church still call her a miracle baby. You can see why your prayer request is special to me, and I will have everyone I know praying for Quincy Rose. Please keep believing, keep praying, and let me know how things are going with her.

"God Bless you all,

A_____"

I have no way to verify this woman's story, but I believe it is true from the tone of her email. But, most importantly, it gave me hope. And when you're feeling desperate, it's so comforting to have stories of hope to hold onto.

Here's another amazing story. This one I found just searching the Internet. I printed it and brought it to our blessing way so that we could keep things in a positive, hopeful light.

Healed in the Womb—Grace's Story

"We thought we would take this opportunity to tell you Grace's story about what God has done for her, and for us this year.

"The story begins when I went for an 18-week ultrasound while pregnant with Grace. They found a large cyst in her brain. We were told it was probably not a really serious type (meaning not likely to kill the baby but with unknown consequences to cognitive and physical function), but we would have to wait two weeks for a subsequent ultrasound for a more definite diagnosis. I could not imagine how there could be such a thing as a non-serious cyst in your unborn child's brain […] I felt the uncertainty over it all was hardest thing to bear, but was soon to discover that the certainty was actually worse […].

"We turned to our Christian family for help. We had close friends praying for us, bible study and prayer groups praying for us […] over that two weeks we became determined we needed to pray for healing.

"When the two weeks were up we returned for a repeat ultrasound to see if we could get some clarification […]

"As they started the scan this time there was no need for talking. We could all see it there, a cyst in the brain that was not only still there, but had grown. We were told that they now believed that our baby did have a really serious cyst, a variant of the Dandy Walker cyst. The cyst was now protruding into the brain under the cerebellum. The favourable things were that there were no other physical abnormalities and no structures in the brain were currently being affected. We were told, however, that it was only a matter of time with the cyst's apparent rate of growth.

"This is a very rare abnormality, only 1 in 30,000 babies. How did this growth of the cyst and a more definitive diagnosis fit in with our conviction that she would be healed? It seems that God wanted to teach us more.

"Things moved very quickly from then. A second opinion the following day confirmed that there was definitely a cyst and it was most likely to be a Dandy-Walker variant. We were told that although very unlikely, the best we could really hope for was that the brain would keep growing and that the cyst would remain the same size, it would not shrink or go away.

"Amniocentesis confirmed that the baby was genetically 100% sound. Some comfort, but these cysts rarely, if ever, have a genetic origin. As we went from one cold doctor's room to another we were introduced to the cold hard facts of medical science as a place often without hope and unfortunately nowadays without even compassion. Termination was offered to us or, alternatively, follow-up with referrals to various support services for families with children with developmental problems.

"There is little research into the condition, but what is available is very discouraging. Ranges of mental and physical disability were discussed, including the fact that our baby may never walk or feed itself. We were shocked to discover that most babies didn't make it to birth, predominantly because they were terminated, others died and those that did make it didn't do well. Over this process our baby was slowly dehumanised.

"As we now better understood the implications of the condition and read and re-read the numerous reports supporting the diagnosis and offering no hope for our child we realised that if anything was going to improve the outcome for our baby, there would be absolutely no doubt that it was God that was doing it. The more hopeless the medical world told us it was, the more we and those supporting us in prayer prayed for healing. We were prepared to accept whatever God was going to do in this situation and bring up the baby as best we could knowing God would be there for us. However, we felt really strongly that we should be praying for healing.

"We had never really understood the power of prayer before this time in our lives even after years of being Christians. Prayer makes a difference. God wants us to pray whether he answers in the way we hope or not. […]

"And God was incredibly gracious and loving, he completely healed our baby.

"At 28 weeks the cyst appeared smaller than the previous ultrasound. By my 30-week scan the cyst was completely gone. The ultrasound technician was stunned and blurted out, "I expected to see a huge cyst in this baby's brain by now."

Three doctors looked for it unsuccessfully. One who hadn't seen us before said, "If I didn't know your history I would have said this is a completely normal scan," which it was—God had healed our unborn baby.

"Since being born, Grace has had two further scans with no sign of any cyst; she has been completely healed […] "We have had people say, 'Oh, well, the equipment sometimes picks things up wrongly' or 'maybe it just went away.' We had a diagnosis, a second opinion, and 8 ultrasounds over a 10-week period showing a growing cyst. There was no doubt by either us or the doctors and ultrasound technicians that the cyst was there. As for it "just going away" it certainly did that against what the medical profession believed would happen. No explanation was offered by the doctors. They just said they were really happy for us […]"

I find it perplexing that there are hardly any miracle stories on the Internet. Or, if there are, I couldn't find them. We heard some word-of-mouth stories from people who had abnormal ultrasound results that turned out to be false. One friend of a friend was told her baby would be born anencephalic (without a forebrain) based on the ultrasound. Fortunately, the baby was born mostly normal, and with a full brain.

When I searched for "bad ultrasound" or "negative ultrasound results" on the Internet, I found articles on people complaining that they wanted a girl though their ultrasound showed a boy or vice versa. When I saw this, it left me fuming. Is this really what people consider a negative ultrasound, getting a girl when you wanted a boy? I'd love to say that I always took the highest spiritual road on this journey with Quincy, and that I was able to let things like this go. I want to just accept people for where they are on their own paths and not feel angry and judgmental. But, unfortunately, I'm not that highly evolved yet. I'm working on it, though. It's a process for us all.

Chapter 17

The Bias of the Blind

Even though we had a very good doctor and a very high tech ultrasound, Dan and I wanted to try another ultrasound. There was always the possibility that the last one was biased because the techs knew why we were sent there in the first place. So we dug deep into our pockets and went to the top spot in San Diego for an independent 3D ultrasound.

This center we went to was not part of any hospital. Most people went there because they had the money to spend and wanted great pictures of their unborn baby. What made this place so unique is that an MD performed the ultrasound and the equipment was the best on the market. When we made the appointment we told them nothing about our previous ultrasounds. We wanted them to perform the ultrasound blind.

"Hi, how are you folks doing? My name is Dr._____. So what brings you to us today?"

"We just wanted to get some great photos of our little Quincy," I lied.

"Okay, great. Please lie back and pull your pants down a little bit and we'll get started," said the young doctor.

In the posh dimly lit room, Quincy's image was suddenly emblazoned on the extra large screen TV mounted on the wall in front of us. The doctor moved the ultrasound probe around my belly in silence.

"Have you ever had an ultrasound before?" he finally spoke.

"Yes," I said curtly.

"What were the results?"

"We just want to know what you see," Dan said edgily.

"Okay, well, it looks like…" and he went into a long description of what we had heard before. Strawberry-shaped head, no esophageal connection with the stomach, small stomach, rocker-bottom feet, clenched hands, three-chamber heart, cleft lip and this time he confirmed a cleft palate.

"I'm so sorry," he said. The ultrasound machine spit out the 3D color photos. "I suppose you don't want these, do you?"

"Yes, I do," I said, not believing someone could be so unthinkingly callous. So she wasn't the perfect conventional little beauty like our other two girls. But we still loved her and I still wanted her photos, even though I knew I wouldn't be able to bring myself to put them on the refrigerator. I didn't want a daily reminder of what was; I wanted to focus on what could be, what would be.

As we left the facility, I sighed heavily to Dan. "I don't know how much more disappointment I can take."

"I know what you mean."

"I really, *really* thought we'd see something different. Something that showed that there was some hope that she wasn't as bad as they first predicted," I said with tears running down my face.

We walked together in silence for a while. The beautiful sunny day with families playing in the park across the street seemed like such a stark contrast to where we were in our own emotional family turmoil.

"But you know what? I still think she's beautiful. Really," I told Dan honestly.

"Me too! Look at that little pug nose. She looks a lot like Willow did in her ultrasound," Dan said.

"I know! I don't know if it's just mother's love or what, but I'm not repulsed or scared of her cleft lip and palate and other deformities at all. I just see our baby, our beautiful Quincy Rose."

When we returned home I sank into a depressed funk. For me a depressed funk looks like nothing is really wrong, except that I easily tear up and don't smile much. I still function and keep busy and take care of myself and those I love. But it felt like I kept pulling myself and my family up, raising our hopes so high, trying so very hard to effect a miracle, to believe a miracle was possible, only to get knocked down by giant tsunami waves of disappointment after disappointment.

How could I keep believing? How could I have faith? What was the point any more? And why did Jesus say in Mark 11:24, "I tell you then, whatever you ask for in prayer, believe that you *have* received it and it *will* be yours" if it wasn't true? How many ways are there to interpret this passage? It seems pretty straightforward to me.

Chapter 18

A Fifth Dimension Being

When I first thought of the idea of making a deal with God I felt a little guilty. Was I trying to force my will by bargaining with my creator? Who was I to do that? But my friend Mehmet said that great spiritual leaders have been doing this since the beginning of time.

The "deal" I asked for out loud was this:

"Dear God, if you heal Quincy and make her healthy, I will write and publish a book about your miracle. I will get an RV and homeschool the kids for a year while we drive around the country sharing the book and your miracle with everyone we meet—people at churches, schools, campgrounds, corporations, bookstore readings, the homeless—anyone and everyone who will listen. I will keep just enough profits from the sales of the books to pay for our gas and food on this journey and donate all the rest to various charities. And in order to boost credibility, if you can heal her cleft lip, I will publish her ultrasound photos in the book. This will be tangible evidence to the world of your miracle."

I felt a little silly saying this aloud, but I really wanted to be heard and I figured this was the best way.

Every day I visualized us walking into Tabitha's school with Quincy strapped to the front of my body in a Baby Bjorn. I pictured myself meeting with the principal and her teacher inside her classroom, handing them a copy of the book. I envisioned explaining to them about our year-long trip and asking them for Tabby's workbooks for the year so that I could homeschool her from the road. I could see this so clearly.

In order to distract ourselves from the depressing ultrasounds, we decided to take a road trip to Sedona, a place of great healing and mystery. I had never been there before but Dan and Tabitha had been there together to visit Dan's brother Tony. The drive was a good distraction. It was breathtakingly beautiful and wondrous how these red rocks jut out of the earth and congregate in this one special place.

Author Debra Katz used to do psychic readings in Sedona. It's a very popular place for massage therapists, and various healers and new age types including psychics. They are attracted by the beauty of the red rock formations and vortex energy. I contacted Debra's assistant to see if I could get a recommendation for a quality psychic in Sedona. Although I agree with Debra that all of us have psychic abilities we can tap into, I feel that many self-proclaimed psychics aren't really that psychically gifted because they don't know how or care to know how to tap into that "claircognizance."

She put me in touch with a woman who does readings from her home. Since we were on the road without a babysitter, we all showed up at her house.

The girls found her home so interesting, full of crystals and feathers and various objects from nature. She had them sit in the living room, allowing them to play with some of the objects while watching TV turned on low.

Our reader was a woman probably in her 60s. She had the distracted demeanor of one who is half in this world and half in some other realm.

"Please have a seat. And feel free to record our session, if you want to. How far along are you?" she asked.

I know that psychics don't know everything all the time, especially when they're not in a relaxed psychic state.

"I'm 31 weeks." That was all I was going to tell her. Dan and I wanted to see what she could come up with on her own.

She began the reading, drawing some deductions that anyone could guess by looking at us before she got into the heart of the reading.

"So how's the baby?" Dan asked pointedly.

"Um, she's fine," she said hesitatingly, playing it close to the vest.

"Do you see anything… special about her?" I asked hopefully.

She inhaled deeply. "Well, I see that she has a sort of an enlarged head…"

Dan and I both got the chills and looked at each other across her kitchen table.

"And it's like she's reaching up to the heavens with her hand, asking for help… " she stopped.

"Please go on. It's okay to tell us whatever you see. We've had some questionable ultrasounds," Dan assured the woman.

"Okay. It feels like she's a fifth-dimension being—like an arcturian or angel, if you believe in that sort of thing, trying to inhabit a third-dimension body. With some difficulty. It's like her energy is too great for her little body."

Fifth-dimension being? I didn't know what she was talking about. Then suddenly I got it.

"Dan!" I interrupted excitedly. "Fifth dimension. Quincy means 'the fifth.' I don't know why we've never talked about that before. I looked it up on the Internet the other day."

"I did, too. Oh my God, you're right. I guess Willow was right. Quincy really is her name."

The reader went on to say that she didn't see Quincy attached to any tubes when she comes out but that her health is frail. And she hasn't yet decided whether she'll stay on earth or go. But she will make it to birth, she assured us.

That night at the hotel I decided to try to do a reading myself. I was excited to do one in Sedona with all of the powerful energy around. Dan and I do these readings from time to time where he asks me questions and I go inward and give answers. We use them as guidance in our lives in various ways. I don't know if it's God or spirits or guardian angels or ancestors who are giving me the information, but it is information from some place other than myself and sometimes it's very accurate and helpful. But not always. The problem is I don't remember a lot of the answers afterwards for some reason. I really need to remember to record them.

We were in the middle of the reading when Tabitha burst into our bedroom.

"What are you guys doing?" she asked curiously.

"Quiet, Tabitha. Mommy is doing a reading. About Quincy."

"Hey, I know… why don't we use the law of attraction to heal Quincy?" Tabitha said. She amazes me sometimes with her understanding of concepts way beyond her age.

"Okay," I said. "Let me see what comes through in the reading."

I closed my eyes and went through the psychic visualization process I had learned. Then I sat and waited patiently for any images to come to me. I saw the Bible open about two-thirds of the way to Mathew 7.

It's rather embarrassing to admit but even though I went to four years of Catholic high school, I learned almost nothing about the Bible. Or I should say I retained nothing. I'm sure they tried to teach us something but I wasn't listening. I was too busy thinking about boys.

"There's a book of Matthew, I know. But where in the Bible is it located?" I asked Dan.

"In the New Testament," Dan said to me incredulously. He has a lot of knowledge about the Bible from his days as a born-again Christian and he can never understand how I know so little about it.

"Ok, well, can you please hand me the Bible in the end table over there. I saw a passage in Matthew 7 but I don't know what it says."

He handed it to me and I started reading aloud. Little of it had any meaning to me until I got to this part (Matthew 7:7-8):

"Ask, and it will be given to you; seek, and you will find; knock, and it will be opened to you. For everyone who asks receives, and the one who seeks finds, and to the one who knocks it will be opened."

I got the chills. This passage is talking about the law of attraction. I didn't even *know* that concept was mentioned in the Bible. Whenever I'm doing a reading and an image comes to me that I know I could not conjure up myself, I know that it has some meaning. But what exactly was the meaning here? Could we heal Quincy using the law of attraction? I know I had been trying to use this principle but was this a sign that we were on the right track?

One question I had been pondering ever since the level 2 ultrasound is where does karma end and co-creation, quantum physics and the law of attraction begin? *Karma* is defined in Hinduism and Buddhism as action, seen as bringing upon oneself inevitable results, good or bad, either in this life or in a reincarnation. If karma exists, then how does it fit in with the theory that you can alter the physical world and create a reality you want? If karma can go back lifetimes, or even if it just exists in this lifetime, how do these theories fit together?

Maybe they don't. Maybe they're just two opposing philosophies, like raw food advocacy versus ayurveda. Both health food theories make sense to me yet they are diametrically opposed to each other: raw versus cooked as being the best and most healthful way to assimilate the maximum amount of nutrients. I can understand how two antithetical theories can exist at the same time but practicing both simultaneously would be impossible. If one is followed, the other must be eschewed. Perhaps when it comes to karma versus co-creating our own reality, maybe whatever theory you believe the most becomes your own personal reality? I didn't have any answers.

I thought about Dan's lost baby from years ago. He only had one day to try to effect a change. The medical team didn't know anything was wrong with her until the day before the scheduled induction. Conversely, we had plenty of time to try to help change Quincy's outcome. I was only 31 weeks. Of course, that was assuming she would make it to full term.

It was during this trip to Sedona when we had a chance to get away from our daily lives that we tried to figure out a plan for her birth. I still wanted to have as natural a childbirth experience as possible, while at the same time keeping in mind that I may need a Caesarean-section or other interventions. But how could I do this at a hospital?

"My friend Karla had two of her babies at a hospital without any epidurals or inductions," I told Dan.

"My sister, too," Dan said.

"Oh, that's right! I forgot about that. But I'm not very strong when I'm giving birth. I feel vulnerable and I go inward. I need an advocate or maybe a doula. But I think I need more than a doula. I need someone who can be a real pain in the ass if I need them to be, someone who can stick up for my wants and needs. Someone like…"

"Tahnee," Dan said.

"Exactly."

Dan's sister Tahnee had a natural birth at a hospital; she would be the perfect choice except for two factors. One, she has two young children that keep her very busy and, two, she lived three hours from the hospital we picked.

Even with those cons, I decided to ask her anyway. If she was meant to do it, she would agree. We called her from Sedona.

"I would be honored to," Tahnee said. It was a relief to know she would be there by my side. Tahnee is an amazing woman—strong, holistically-oriented, assertive yet smart and polite. She would handle this well.

"I want to do a natural birth at the hospital but if there comes a point when it's not safe, I'm ready to give in to medical interventions. But only if it's absolutely necessary."

"I understand completely. I'll be there for you," Tahnee assured me.

"Are you sure it's not too much with work and the girls and the distance? I don't want to put you out."

"It's no problem at all. I spoke with Brad and he's ready to leave work and get the girls at any time."

"You know there's a chance she won't live. I'm worried about Dan, what his reaction might be after losing Brianna. He seems so strong but he may have feelings come up that are overwhelming if this birth takes a similar path. You being there will help greatly, but do you think you can handle the possibility that she may be a stillbirth or not live very long?"

"Yes. I can be there for you and be strong. But make sure you get to hold her for a while after she's born, regardless of what they tell you her condition is," Tahnee explained. She knew of a woman who held her baby pronounced dead upon birth, and the baby came back to life. Here is the article:

"It was a final chance to say goodbye for grieving mother Kate Ogg after doctors gave up hope of saving her premature baby. She tearfully told her lifeless son—born at 27 weeks weighing 2 pounds—how much she loved him and cuddled him tightly, not wanting to let him go. Although little Jamie's twin sister Emily had been delivered successfully, doctors had given Mrs. Ogg the news all mothers dread—that after 20 minutes of battling to get her son to breathe, they had declared him dead.

"Having given up on a miracle, Mrs Ogg unwrapped the baby from his blanket and held him against her skin. And then an extraordinary thing happened. After two hours of being hugged, touched and spoken to by his mother, the little boy began showing signs of life.

"At first, it was just a gasp for air that was dismissed by doctors as a reflex action.

"But then the startled mother fed him a little breast milk on her finger and he started breathing normally.

"I thought, 'Oh my God, what's going on,' said Mrs. Ogg.

"A short time later he opened his eyes. It was a miracle. Then he held out his hand and grabbed my finger.

"He opened his eyes and moved his head from side to side. The doctor kept shaking his head saying, 'I don't believe it, I don't believe it.'

"The Australian mother spoke publicly for the first time yesterday to highlight the importance of skin-on-skin care for sick babies, which is being used at an increasing number of British hospitals.

"In most cases, babies are rushed off to intensive care if there is a serious problem during the birth.

"But the 'kangaroo care' technique, named after the way kangaroos hold their young in a pouch next to their bodies, allows the mother to act as a human incubator to keep babies warm, stimulated, and fed.

"Pre-term and low birth-weight babies treated with the skin-to-skin method have also been shown to have lower infection rates, less severe illness, improved sleep patterns and are at reduced risk of hypothermia.

"Mrs. Ogg and her husband David told how doctors gave up on saving their son after a three-hour labour in a Sydney hospital in March.

"'The doctor asked me had we chosen a name for our son,' said Mrs. Ogg. 'I said, 'Jamie,' and he turned around with my son already wrapped up and said, 'We've lost Jamie, he didn't make it, sorry.' It was the worse feeling I've ever felt. I unwrapped Jamie from his blanket. He was very limp.'

"'I took my gown off and arranged him on my chest with his head over my arm and just held him. He wasn't moving at all and we just started talking to him. We told him what his name was and that he had a sister. We told him the things we wanted to do with him throughout his life. Jamie occasionally gasped for air, which doctors said was a reflex action. But then I felt him move as if he were startled, then he started gasping more and more regularly. I gave Jamie some breast milk on my finger, he took it and started regular breathing.'

"Mrs. Ogg held her son, now five months old and fully recovered, as she spoke on the Australian TV show *Today Tonight*. Her husband added: 'Luckily I've got a very strong, very smart wife. She instinctively did what she did. If she hadn't done that, Jamie probably wouldn't be here.'"

[To see the article online, go to http://www.dailymail.co.uk/health/article-1306283/Miracle-premature-baby-declared-dead-doctors-revived-mothers-touch.html#axzz2KF3Icytx.]

Chapter 19

Heroics and Other Euphemisms

I thought about how a 12- or 13-year-old girl would handle this situation. If over 40 and under 18 are the main high-risk age categories for women to have trisomy 18 babies, how could a child with such limited life experience handle this? I was glad to be over 40 in this case. When devastating news happens in our lives, it gives us the opportunity to put life into perspective and not sweat about the petty grievances. The challenge is to carry this perspective with us after the storm has passed.

Like can produce more like and in this case our collective emotional turmoil created more turmoil with regard to finding a safe and suitable doctor and venue to handle our unique situation with Quincy. We kept getting the run-around from doctors. Actually, we don't know if it was the doctors themselves or their offices screwing up and not getting messages to them. But we could not get a couple of doctors to return our many calls. I don't know if it was because we were on Medi-Cal insurance or because they didn't want to deal with the emotional issues related to this delivery. Either it was risky for them because they didn't know how we would react to her birth or because they were perhaps uneasy about their own reactions. It's much more fun delivering plump and healthy little babies, I'd imagine.

In any case, we ended up with the doctor who did our level 2 ultrasound. But before we wound up with him, one doctor that we met with reviewed our ultrasound and agreed with the findings that Quincy had trisomy 18.

"We're not going to do any heroics here, are we?" he pushed, looking at us from over top of his reading glasses. "Heroics" was the common euphemism we found doctors using to mean doing everything possible to help our baby live after birth.

"Yes, we are," Dan stood his ground. "This is our baby and we want you to do everything you can to give her a chance at life."

"But these babies don't make it past birth usually. They never live past their teens. And those who do make it to their teens have to be institutionalized," he ignorantly tried to inform us. "I'd recommend comfort care."

"Comfort care" was another euphemism we heard often. It means "do nothing but hold your baby until she dies."

"I don't care. She's alive and you need to keep her that way if she's born alive," Dan asserted.

The doctor never returned any of our calls after that day.

Chapter 20

Searching for Roots on a Farm

It's been about a month since I began writing this story. Ever since the day we hit the road for Maine I've kept asking myself: Why Maine? Why now? I never pictured myself living here. I never gave Maine a thought. I understand the circumstances that prompted our move, of course, but why did it end up being Maine of all the possible choices? Besides Tabitha informing us that living in a place where it snows a lot is her "lifelong dream," the answer about why we're in Maine still isn't completely clear to me.

I keep waiting for that moment when it becomes very apparent. A chance meeting with someone that alters our life paths. Or perhaps a new opportunity that is unique to Maine. Or maybe a disaster averted. Dan and I were watching the news last night and there was a segment about global climate change. They showed a map of the continental US and how almost all of the states had experienced five times the number of record high temperatures as record low temperatures in 2012. All the states except for Maine, that is.

Dan suggested the idea that maybe it has nothing to do with us but with future generations in our family who grow up here.

It is becoming clearer why circumstances aligned to boot us out of Julian, even if just temporarily. Babies. Many of my friends in Julian are pregnant and having babies. My first reaction when I hear that a friend is pregnant is complete joy for them. I'm not at all envious. I have no desire to be pregnant again—ever. This is healthy for me, I think. Because I love having children so much that I'd probably just keep trying to have babies until it was too late. I guess that's what I did do.

But as soon as I hear a friend's baby is born, I feel envy. It's made me realize that I don't want to be pregnant but I still want the prize. Maybe we'll adopt soon, after a year has passed. I know that children choose us so I'm leaving it up to God or fate. A Native American friend of mine in Julian lost her sister suddenly several years ago. In her tribe, it is customary to do nothing for a year. No major changes or decisions. Not even changing jobs. And no exercise. Time is needed for mourning and healing. I guess I haven't fully heeded that advice. I think my tribe is nomadic.

After Tabitha was born, I felt very restless. We were living in an apartment complex near the beach, surrounded by 20-somethings who would come home rowdy at 2 a.m. after a night of drinking and other debauchery. We were a family and we needed a real home. But how could we afford one?

We really wanted a farm. This would be a safe and interesting place to raise a family. We searched on eBay for owner-financed land in California. The only place we found land that wasn't arid desert was in inland Northern California in a small town called Alturas. We put a small down payment on the parcel, contingent on seeing the property. We packed up our new baby and hit the road.

After a couple of hours into the drive I realized that taking a road trip a month after giving birth with a third-degree tear was not such a great idea. I was in pain. I purchased a donut cushion for the ride and sat in the back seat with Tabitha. It didn't help much but made the drive a little more tolerable. Even though my bottom was very sore, I so enjoyed playing with her. She'd smile at me, wrinkling up her little nose as if to say, "Isn't this the most fun?! We get to sit together!" I played a Baby Einstein musical car carrier toy for her over and over again, and toyed with her little monkey toes.

When we finally arrived in Alturas, we made our way in the dark to a small and eerie cabin Dan had rented for us at the bottom of the mountain subdivision. As we approached the cabin I realized we were out of cell service range.

"Dan, I can't do this! What if something happens or Tabitha needs a doctor or something?"

"She's fine. It's just for one night," he tried to assure me.

"I can't do it. I'm sorry," I said. I was a very overwhelmed and nervous new mom. Dan humored me and we got a hotel room in town instead.

The next day we had breakfast at a restaurant and drove around town to check things out before heading up the mountain to the property. Alturas is a very isolated small town in the northeastern part of California. At first glance, it seemed to be very nice and safe, the kind of place where you could leave your doors unlocked and let your kids run around the neighborhood.

But this isn't exactly where we had bought property. Our parcel was in a mountain subdivision called California Pines, the planners of which apparently had great hopes and designs for it that never quite panned out. Perhaps one day, if more people move to Alturas, but when we were there it was pretty sparsely populated. To get to the property you had to drive up a very long winding road and past our would-be neighbor, Bunker Bob.

Bunker Bob had this moniker for a very good reason—his property looked like the makeshift bunker of one who is a bit paranoid. I'll just leave it at that. As we slowly drove past his place to take a look, his pack of dogs ran out into the street and surrounded our vehicle.

It was quite a while ago and I don't exactly remember our conversation with Mr. Bob. He was a nice person but judging from his dwelling, it was probably heavily armed. Not really the kind of neighbor you want, especially when he's your only neighbor and you want to set up a farm and raise kids.

We found the property about a mile down the road and it took us several pass-bys to figure out which was ours. It was difficult to determine because it was a wooded lot on what seemed to be a parcel almost as steep as a cliff.

"Although berming into a hill won't be a problem, I don't really see us building an Earthship here and farming, do you?" I asked Dan, knowing what his response would be. Dan, very disappointed, said, "Yeah, you're right. Well, let me hike down there and take a full look. It is seven acres. Maybe there's a flat spot somewhere."

Dan scaled the cliff, between dense beautiful trees, and thoroughly checked out the land. I stayed back and held onto Tabitha, keeping one eye out for anything or anyone dangerous.

"Back to Carlsbad," Dan said. "This is such a bummer. The pictures did not show how steep this is."

"Good thing there's a clause in there about getting our money back if we don't like it." And so we did.

A year later, when Tabitha turned one, we gave it another try—this time in Hawaii. Why Hawaii, besides the obvious natural beauty? I had some ties there. My sister was living in Maui at the time. My grandparents had lived on Oahu during the attack on Pearl Harbor and my dad was born there soon after. Also, it is not widely known, but very affordable land can be had on parts of Hawaii Island, better known as The Big Island.

Again we turned to eBay as that's the place to go when you're looking for owner-financed land. We didn't find exactly what we wanted but we gathered enough information to know that it would be a place where we could find affordable land owner-financed.

Having learned somewhat from our last mistake, we thought it best to rent on the island and take our time searching for the right parcel.

Dan flew over there first and found a rental for us in Volcano. As the name suggests, Volcano is a town that is, well, on top of a volcano—Kilauea, the longest flowing volcano in the world. Most Hawaiian people will not live in Volcano because traditionally it is a place only for royalty. The fear is that you will upset Pele, goddess of the volcano, along with fire, lightning, and wind. And probably because who wants to be that close to a volcano when it is erupting?

It is an amazing place, though. About 4,000 feet above sea level, it is cold at night and cool during the day in the winter. There's a range of types of houses there: everything from farms to modest houses in subdivisions to mansions buried deep in the jungle.

We enjoyed living in Volcano while we looked for our piece of land. We wanted something that was at least a few acres so that we could build a farm.

After just five months we found four acres owner financed on the Hilo side of the island in a subdivision called Fern Acres. It was a thick jungle of mostly low brush. The front part of the subdivision consisted of tall trees and most of the parcels were at least a couple of acres. The back part of the subdivision, where we purchased land, had been covered by lava years earlier and was still in a process of regrowth.

We hired our new friend Mehmet to use his backhoe to clear a path into our jungle. You couldn't even really walk very far into the property without some help clearing the brush. Mehmet leveled a spot for us to set up a temporary off-grid structure. Our plan was to save money by living on the property while slowly building our permanent home as we could afford it, without seeking a mortgage.

We put considerable thought into what kind of structure we could live in and be comfortable in for a few years. Since the temperature on this part of the island was warm, we had plenty of flexibility. Although it is one of the rainiest spots on the planet, we figured that would work to our advantage as we could set up a water catchment system instead of having to drill a well or hook up with a municipal water supply.

We definitely weren't the only people to do this on the island. Some people lived in yurts, others in makeshift tents. Some people converted old school buses while others purchased shipping containers and converted them into living quarters. And although there were some rules in place, Hawaii Island generally wasn't too strict about enforcing building permits or regulating temporary structures.

Since Dan was doing tire export at the time he had a contact in China who was able to procure a military tent for us at a good price. This tent was military green and looked like something from *M*A*S*H*. It wasn't beautiful to look at, but it was very functional and gave us 512 square feet of living space. We figured if we needed more space later, we could always get another tent and connect the two.

While waiting for it to be shipped, we prepared the ground with cinder. Leveling was a very important step so we went to Home Depot to gather some supplies, such as stakes.

"Why are these stakes so short?" I asked a sales clerk. I had never seen wooden stakes like these. They were maybe a foot or a foot and a half long.

"Because there's only a few inches of topsoil on most of the island. You don't need them to be long," he said, looking at me like I was a bit daft.

This never occurred to us before we moved there. We wanted to farm and we just thought we'd easily level the land and build. But since this was very new earth, what was under the topsoil was hard lava tubes. And those were not so easy to flatten and move. In fact, the only way to build a permanent structure on this property would be to hire someone to come in with a huge excavator. The land was so full of jungle undergrowth and lava tubes that I never was able to walk the four acres the whole time we lived there. Dan tried one day with our dog, Buddy, and they almost got lost. They were both completely exhausted by the time they returned home.

The next big task was to search the island for free wooden shipping pallets. Whenever we spotted wooden pallets with blue spray paint on the ends, we knew those were the strong ones and we'd ask if we could have them. We were able to gather enough to manufacture a floor for the tent, cover it with plywood and then linoleum. It looked just like a floor you would find in many conventional homes and it was quite sturdy.

After Dan and Mehmet erected the tent, I went to work decorating the interior. I covered the walls with handmade woven leaf mats and the ceiling with colorful leaf-print fabric. I was going for a *Gilligan's Island* look. I put framed pictures of our family, mostly baby pictures of Tabitha, on all the tent walls. I draped a mosquito net over our beds for a functional and romantic look.

Dan built a cylinder-shaped water catchment out of large rice bags. He stuffed the bags with cinder rock and held them in place by snagging them with barbed wire between each layer. We draped the inside of the water catchment with a very large plastic food-grade water catchment liner. When it rained, water would run off of the pitched roof of the tent, into the rain gutters that Dan had installed and pour straight to the back of the tent and into our water catchment.

We even had a place to do laundry. Dan set up a shed next to the tent with a washer and dryer and connected it and all of our indoor electrical needs to a bank of marine batteries, an inverter, and a gas-powered generator. How he knew how to do this was a mystery to me. Dan is great at figuring things out; he's an incredibly creative problem solver. Usually his expertise is limited to his trade, the automotive industry. But in this case he stretched himself into new territory.

On the inside we sectioned off each area of the tent to make it seem like a real home with somewhat separate rooms. In the far left corner we set up a composting toilet, sink, and claw-foot bathtub with a showerhead. In the far right corner of the tent we set up Tabitha's closet and crib. The entire back section of the tent was separated by a line of six-feet-tall plastic Rubbermaid-type closets in which we stored our clothes, dishes, kitchenware, etc.

Next to the row of closets was our dining table and perpendicular to the table in the center of the tent was our king-sized bed. The refrigerator, kitchen sink, stove, and counters were on the other side of the tent opposite our bed. The front of the tent was our living room, which we partitioned with couches. Across from the L-shaped couches were a small desk, computer, toy bins, and TV.

As you can imagine, we utilized every square inch of the tent. I loved the tent, at first. When we moved in, it had the muffled silence of a new snowfall. Being in the middle of the jungle in a tent without any noisy traffic around was pure bliss.

We obtained a few chickens and three goats to start off our menagerie. And a rooster. One morning at about 4 or 5 a.m. the rooster stood next to our "bedroom" tent flap and tried to cock-a-doodle-doo. It literally sounded like someone was standing outside our tent pretending to sound like a rooster. It was the most bizarre noise. But it was just our adolescent rooster trying out his new vocal chords. I was about seven months pregnant with Willow at the time and hardly thrilled about the rooster waking me up from much needed sleep!

As a nature girl or "wild animal girl" as she calls herself, Tabitha loved living in the tent. It was an adventure. I loved the adventure, too, until some uncomfortable realities set in. Such as rain and lightning. On one of our first nights in the tent we suddenly realized we had forgotten to ground it. We weren't really sure how much it mattered because if lightning struck there, it would cut through the tent like butter, anyway. On this night, there was an electrical storm unlike any I've ever experienced. Rolling waves of continuous lightning and thunder shot through the night sky without pause. Dan and I huddled in bed together with Tabitha, praying we'd make it through the night alive.

After the storm passed, every night I'd take Tabitha out onto the front porch and watch the stars before I'd tuck her into her crib. They were amazing. One night we even saw a moonbow—a nighttime version of a rainbow. They are very rare and usually only seen in rainy climates like Hilo.

Every night I'd get up to pee several times, as pregnant women do, and I'd look out our bathroom tent flap at the glow of the lava flow in the distance. It was very beautiful and since it was far away and downhill from us, I figured it wasn't much of a threat. (The last lava flow here came from a different and currently dormant volcano.) But it was a bit disconcerting to notice that the glow of the lava flow would markedly shift directions each night. Sometimes I could see it from the front of the tent and the next night it would be in a completely different place.

The goats were always good for entertainment. We found them for free on Craigslist. We picked them up on Easter weekend on the other side of the island, near Kona. As Dan was loading the goats into our pickup, I was watching Tabitha play in the yard. I noticed that she was getting close to the top of this pretty steep hill so I tried to call her back. She started running down a steep driveway that ended on a street. She was out of control as if she were stumbling and about to fall and roll down the hill.

Panicked, I sprinted after her as fast as a pregnant woman can. Instinctively, I dove forward reaching my right hand out as far as possible, just barely snagging her arm. I threw her back up the hill and did a shoulder roll, missing a direct hit to Willow in my belly. I was bloody and dirty, covered in road rash on one side of my body. The next day I had Willow checked by my midwife and, thankfully, she was fine. It's amazing what a maternal instinct can propel us to do.

The goats were helpful to some extent as they ate a lot of the underbrush, so we gave them free rein. Sometimes they would come marching into the tent and into the kitchen as if to say, "Hey, what's for lunch?"

Tabitha always had a piece of nature in her hand, whether she was indoors or outside. One day she had a stick in each hand as she played on the front porch. The oldest and largest goat was standing on the other side of the porch opposite Tabitha. Tabitha, who wasn't even two years old at the time, walked toward the sharp-horned goat. The goat must have thought Tabitha looked like another horned goat who wanted to fight or play. So she backed up and took a running leap towards Tabitha, horns down and ready to skewer her.

Again, motherly instinct leapt into action and I scooped up Tabby just in time. Later that day, we bought two small rubber balls and super glued them to the tip of each horn. She looked adorable.

The next day there was a sudden torrential rain. The sky was sunny the moment before and it came on quickly, catching us all off guard. We were used to the afternoon rains but this one was very strong. We had a little dog house just outside the tent for Buddy and he usually hung out there all day. When the downpour began, the goats immediately sought cover in Buddy's dog house, forcing Buddy to evacuate the premises. Buddy, being the nice dog that he is, just sat outside his house in the rain, allowing the goats to take over his space.

When the goats ran out of easy-access underbrush, they decided to eat our tent. So we let the chickens out of the coop and tethered the goats instead. The chickens were so cute with their babies huddled under their feathers. They looked like children hiding under a mother's long skirt.

Living in Hawaii was definitely an interesting experience, quite different from just visiting there as a tourist. I found the Hawaiian people to be in one of two camps: either truly living the *aloha* spirit as being the nicest and most generous people you could ever meet or prejudicial wanting non-natives off their island. Most, in my experience, were in the latter camp, unfortunately. For example, we would often see bumper stickers in Hawaii that said *Kau Inoa*. This is a movement by the Hawaiian people to bring people of Hawaiian descent back to the islands. That made sense to me. But part of this movement includes setting up a separate government where only people of Hawaiian ancestry would be allowed to run for office and vote.

One day I took Tabitha and Buddy to a park in Volcano. I was a few weeks pregnant with Willow and very fuzzy-headed and queasy. I had forgotten to pack some baggies for picking up Buddy's poop. So, of course, Buddy crapped in the park, though right at the edge of the woods so that no one would be likely to step in it, leaving it to turn to compost in no time in the rainy climate.

An older Hawaiian woman made a beeline across the field towards me.

"Hello," I said pleasantly, wondering what she wanted that could be so important to cause her to walk headlong over to me.

"Clean up that shit!" she screamed at me.

"I'm sorry, I forgot to bring baggies. I'm pregnant and not really all there lately," I explained.

"I don't care. You can't bring your dog here and let him shit all over the place. Who do you think cleans that up?" She was standing about six inches from my face and I was beginning to panic as we were the only people in the park. I felt like she was going to strike me.

"I said I'm sorry," I reiterated.

As she turned angrily to walk away, I gathered up my nerve and dander.

"What is your name?" I demanded. "I'm sure your boss would love to know how you speak to people."

"You don't own this park," she said.

"I know. Neither do you. Who owns a park?"

"Local people," she said haughtily.

I later learned that this was code for people with Hawaiian blood. Even though my father was born in Hawaii, that didn't count. He's white.

I was trying to earn some money to help our family out while still being a full-time stay-at-home mother. So I sold Avon. The woman who recruited me was Mexican American from California. Her husband was Caucasian. As an Avon representative in a leadership position, she would hold large meetings at her home on a regular basis. The local women would assume she was Hawaiian because of the color of her skin. When they came to the meetings they would ask suspiciously, "Who's the white guy in the corner?"

"My husband," she simply replied. She called it reverse discrimination. I think it's simply discrimination. Even though I hated being treated with prejudice, in retrospect it was a really good experience to live in a place where we were the minority. It made me more sensitive to people on the mainland in the same situation. I also discovered from this period that I prefer living in more of a melting pot area. I guess we're not really experiencing that in Northern Maine, though.

Although I didn't really make much money, I enjoyed selling Avon. I loved the smell of the brochures and the social aspects of the job. But after trying many of the products out, I realized I couldn't sell something that made my skin break out. I did like some of the perfumes and other products, though.

Chapter 21

Enter Willow, Stage Left

Before Willow was born we considered having a home water birth in the tent but we were a good half hour to the nearest hospital, which made me nervous. So we opted to birth at a women's center on the opposite side of the island. It was kind of like a birth center, but not as homey. When I went in for a routine appointment in my ninth month, they found me to be dilated a couple of centimeters but not enough to admit me.

"Go home or stay at a hotel across the street, it's your choice," the midwife said. "It could be later today or a week from now, so hard to say."

We had left Tabitha at her preschool near home so staying at a hotel was not an option. We drove the two-hour winding trek through the country back to Hilo, arriving at around sunset. At a stoplight in town the car listed to the right. We had a flat. It was such bad timing because all the tire shops had just closed for the evening. Hilo is still a rather small town and businesses rarely stay open very late. Dan's tire equipment was being shipped over to the island but wasn't due to arrive until the next week. So he put a donut on the Saturn and we continued our drive home to pick up Tabitha.

"This isn't good. What if I go into labor tonight? Should we really make the drive to the other side of the island on a donut, through those winding hills?" I asked Dan.

Unfortunately, we had just sold our gas-guzzling truck a week earlier because we couldn't afford the gas for it when it prices spiked to $4.50 per gallon. We were mostly together all the time anyway, so we figured we could get around better in Dan's economical Saturn.

We picked up Tabitha and had our evening as usual. After we put her to bed I was feeling restless. I couldn't sleep so I played around on the computer while Tab and Dan slept. I started to get that undeniable cramping feeling of contractions or "pressure waves" as my Hypnobabies course had taught me to call them.

I walked over to the mosquito net-draped bed and poked my husband. "Dan, wake up. It's time." It was about 11:30 p.m.

He rallied quickly, packing up my suitcase and a confused Tabitha into the car. Willow wasn't due for another three weeks so I wasn't quite as packed as I had wanted to be.

As we approached Hilo on our way to the women's center, I decided to call them and touch base, letting them know we were coming. But the pressure waves were becoming stronger and more frequent. I wasn't feeling too sure about the long drive over there, especially on a donut. What if I couldn't make it and had to birth on the side of the road or in someone's farm house? Although I'm sure I wouldn't be the first woman to do that here, it was not my desired outcome.

"You'll be fine," the first midwife assured me. "Just take your time. We'll be here for you when you get here."

I hung up. More pressure waves, more discomfort. More worry.

"Dan, I don't know about this. Let me call them again."

A different midwife answered. I explained to her about my trepidation.

"Why don't you go to Hilo Hospital and get checked," she said calmly. "If you're not too dilated, you can continue on."

That seemed like a reasonable idea. But I would not be staying at that hospital because I had heard so many horror stories about it from the locals. Dan pulled the Saturn into the emergency lane, turned off the engine for a moment and assisted me and Tabitha out of the vehicle.

"Where are her shoes?" Dan asked me. Tabitha ran into the hospital barefoot, enamored with a giant colorful *honu* or "sea turtle" sculpture in the lobby.

"I'm about to give birth here. I don't think it's my responsibility to make sure she has shoes!"

We kept calling our babysitter but couldn't get hold of her. We called a neighbor instead. It was a little after midnight.

"Can you come down to the hospital and take Tabitha with you?" Dan asked.

"No… I'm really tired. I don't think I can make the drive."

It was only a half hour away. I was hoping this was code for "I'm too stoned to drive your daughter anywhere," not just an incredibly selfish moment.

A few weeks earlier we had asked two of Dan's co-workers if they could be our backup sitters in case something happened to our sitter when I went into labor. Dan worked as a sales representative for a large tire chain on the island before he decided to quit and go into business for himself.

"Nah, I don't think so."

"Okay," Dan said, waiting for the polite excuse to follow that never came. The next day he asked the receptionist.

"No, I don't want to," she said. And so that was that.

As I checked into my room at the hospital, Dan was dragging Tabitha back to the car screaming.

"Nooooo, I want to see the turtle!"

"Come on, Tabitha. We have to move our car. It's parked in the emergency lane and we *have* to get it out of there."

Dan finally wrestled Tabitha into her car seat. He tried to turn the key in the ignition, but the Saturn would not start. This had never happened to this car before. We were stuck. I was going to birth at Hilo Hospital.

Finally, around 3 a.m., we located our babysitter who picked up Tabitha and whisked her away.

A woman in the room next to me was screaming in agony in the most tortured scream I had ever heard. Dan was down in the parking lot with Tabitha, helping our sitter with the car seat.

"What's wrong with her?" I asked the nurse.

"She just got her epidural too late."

That settled it. Screw the hypnosis. I'd had too much stress for one day. I took the epidural.

Dan was there by my side as the labor continued. We made sure there were no other interventions; we wanted her to come out on her own time. But as she lowered into my pelvis, her heartbeat dropped precipitously.

"Where's the doctor?" Dan yelled.

"She's in the hall. I'll get her." The doctor was on the phone and didn't want to leave her conversation.

"Doctor? Doctor?" the nurse said, too patiently and politely considering what was going on in our room.

"Mr. Marsh," the nurse turned to Dan and said firmly, "I need to know that if we tell you to leave the room, you will."

"Why? What is going on?"

Backpedaling, the nurse made an effort to reassure us and keep us calm.

"Don't worry, Willow is just making a dramatic entrance. She'll be a drama queen one day."

And she was right. Willow is very dramatic today, in speech and mannerisms.

Finally the doctor hung up and came into our room. She pushed Willow back in a little bit because the cord was wrapped around her neck.

"I need a c-section, don't I?" I asked the doctor.

"Well, yes, but there's no one here who can do one. We have already paged the doctor and he's coming but there's another woman ahead of you who needs one," the doctor said matter-of-factly.

Strangely, I was not panicked. This was one of those moments where you just know there's nothing you can really do and you just have to surrender to whatever help you can get around you or from above.

"What should I do?" I asked.

And I'll never forget what she said: "Just push her out."

It was almost humorous. I may as well have been in the tent. I would have had better support there. So I just pushed her out. They turned off the epidural and I pushed so hard and fast as if my baby's life depended on it—because it did. And out she came, pink and perfect.

A few hours later, my brother called offering his congratulations. He reminded me that Willow was born on Little G's birthday. Amidst the chaos, I hadn't even realized my daughter was born on my grandmother's birthday, three weeks before her due date.

Chapter 22

Coincidences and Realities

During my pregnancy with Quincy I noticed a strange bump on my forehead that seemed to surface out of nowhere. It continued to grow at an alarming rate. My family doctor looked at it and declared that it most likely was a squamous cell carcinoma.

"Better have that biopsied and taken off at UCSD," he said with a slightly concerned look.

"Is it something to worry about?" I asked. I did not need another source of anxiety, but for better or for worse it was a distraction from my pregnancy concerns.

"No… but you will need to get it removed as soon as possible."

My doctor said it could take a few weeks to a few months to be seen, so I called the next day to make an appointment.

"UCSD Medical Center, this is Quincy, how may I help you?" asked a friendly young woman.

"Quincy? Wow, what a coincidence; that's my baby's name. You don't meet many female Quincys, do you?" I asked.

"No, you don't. I've never met one," said Quincy.

When I hung up I wondered about the odds. What were the odds of a squamous cell tumor popping up on my forehead during pregnancy leading me to call a healthcare provider for treatment where a female Quincy works? And this woman had lived her whole life and never met or heard of another female Quincy. Perhaps I was reading too much into it, but nevertheless I found it fascinating.

I had read in *You Are Psychic* that we should pay attention to any thoughts or songs we hear when we first awake. They could be messages to us from the spirit world. The past few mornings I found myself waking up to *The Last Unicorn* song refrain, "I'm alive, I'm alive," in my head. I thought maybe it was Quincy reminding me that she was still here and still important. I was hoping it was a message from her telling me that she would be born alive, but I wasn't sure.

One morning I woke up and the name Eckhart Tolle was on my mind. I hadn't thought about this author in a long time nor had I read any of his books. But I remembered that Dan had read *The Power of Now* when we were living in Hawaii. Since I was open to most positive messages and signs, I decided to get a copy of it from the library, the CD version. I found it to be very esoteric but also quite helpful and comforting, reminding me to live in the moment, not the past, not the future. Maybe it was another message from somewhere helping me to cope with carrying a special baby like Quincy. The message to be present seemed to me to be coming through clearly.

During this time of waiting, nurturing, and nesting, I had a phone consultation with a lactation specialist. She was incredibly knowledgeable and came highly recommended by my friend Lydia. I had had some breast-feeding challenges in the past so this time I wanted to make sure I would be prepared for Quincy. And since the ultrasound showed she had a cleft lip and possibly a cleft palate, I knew that if that were true she and I would both need special assistance, possibly more than the hospital would be able to provide.

Every day I continued to do and expand my visualizations. One of my favorites was picturing driving home from the hospital with Dan, Quincy in her car seat and me in the back seat with her. We'd pull up to the house, park, and I'd unstrap her from her car seat. Dan's parents and the girls would be waiting excitedly for us on the front porch. I'd bring her inside with everyone oohing and ahhing over her, wanting to touch her, see her. I'd sit quietly on the couch and ask the girls to go wash their hands. I pictured myself laying her on the Boppy as I breastfed her. Sometimes when I'd picture this she would look perfect; other times she'd have a cleft lip. But she was always healthy overall.

If the ultrasounds were correct, though, the reality would be quite different. My neighbor, Renee, a former nurse, described what the picture might really look like.

"I can come over to help, if you want. She's going to need it quiet here; she'll be very frail."

How could that happen, I wondered. My house is always very noisy and messy.

"I can help show you how to intubate her. I've taught families how to do this before. And we can practice ahead of time, showing the girls what it will be like by using one of their dolls as an example."

Intubate? The other reality was beginning to set in. What outcome did I really want here? What outcome was I willing to accept? And did I have any choice? If she were born highly disabled, only eating from a tube her whole life, would I accept her? Of course I would and of course I'd love her. But could I *handle* it? I'm the kind of person who gets nervous diarrhea every time one of my girls gets the flu. And how much time, love, and attention would Quincy's extra care take away from Willow and Tabitha? Would there be money and time to continue to take them to dance classes? Or for hikes on the weekends and to the movies? And what about my relationship with Dan? Would we go out on the rare date night ever again?

It was time to get soul-searchingly honest with myself. Let's assume a miracle didn't happen and Quincy was what everyone in the medical community had been telling us, T18, I asked myself what would be a better outcome for me and my family, and for Quincy? Death or life? Not that I had any control over this. Death would be devastating for our family for sure, whether it were to occur while I was still carrying her or shortly thereafter. But what about life? A life that would make other disabilities look easy? I felt so guilty feeling these feelings and thinking these thoughts about my baby, asking these questions you're not supposed to ask.

I was prepared mentally and emotionally—although not practically—to take care of her no matter how sick and disabled she might be. But a part of me, a selfish or pragmatic part of me, knew that death would probably be the best outcome for all involved. But how did I know this for sure? If she arrived and lived and was very sick/disabled, wouldn't I love her just as much as I do Tabitha and Willow, more and more each day? Would it matter at all how much time, effort, money, and energy it took out of us? Would it feel like something being extracted from us or would it feel rewarding as if having done a good deed, but magnified because we loved her so much? Of course I loved Quincy at this point but there's something so much more tangible about the love I feel when a baby is in my arms, not just my belly. I wondered if other women felt this way.

Chapter 23

A Human Incubator

It was early February and my belly was swelling more than it should for the number of weeks I was pregnant. Tabitha had suddenly taken a great interest in Quincy. She was talking to my belly all the time and getting very excited about her arrival. She would chatter about all the things she wanted to do with Quincy. I worried about her excited anticipation, hoping that she would be able to play with her sister and not have to deal with the crushing disappointment and sadness of a sister who didn't survive. I was wondering if I had made the right decision, giving everyone such hope, especially the children who don't understand all the possibilities.

Then one evening out of nowhere, Willow said to me, "Mommy, you're going to jail."

I didn't know what she was talking about and just blew it off as one of those funny things kids say. The next day I found out what she meant.

We went as a family to shop at an outdoor mall. I was feeling very big and uncomfortable that day, too uncomfortable for being just 31 weeks pregnant. I had a sense something was wrong but I didn't want to voice it out loud and make it real. I kept stopping to rest. Dan was getting irritated with me. I think he knew something was up, too, and it scared him.

That evening Dan and I put the kids to bed as usual but we slept in the living room on our bed. We were painting our bedroom for Quincy's arrival. Dan wanted a bright happy color on the wall to stimulate her and make her want to stay with us.

As we watched TV, I couldn't get into a comfortable position on our bed. This may not sound that unusual for a pregnant woman, but I was extremely uncomfortable with a major side cramp and, again, I was only 31 weeks. It had become so bad that I could hardly move. I didn't feel like I was in labor, but something wasn't right.

"Dan, I think I need to go to the hospital and get checked."

We decided he should stay home with the kids until morning and our neighbor Renee, the former nurse, would drive me to the hospital an hour and 15 minutes away. The drive was through some winding mountain roads, sometimes with spotty cell service. Although we hadn't asked her ahead of time or even planned for her to drive me, we figured I was safest with her.

When we got to the hospital medical tests determined there was a 95% chance I would deliver soon unless I stayed on bed rest there. I never found out exactly what the side cramping was all about, but with all the poking and prodding my body started going into active, painful labor. It's always painful when you're scared.

Renee stayed with me for a couple of hours until they transferred me to the Perinatal Special Care Unit. The hospital's goal was to keep Quincy inside of me for as long as possible—at least until 33 weeks, when the chance for survival outside of my womb would be greatest.

"You're the best incubator there is," one doctor told me. And that's exactly just what I felt like, an incubator.

Round-the-clock monitoring ensued with an IV of magnesium sulfate. This is basically Epsom salts suspended in liquid being pumped into your body. It's a muscle relaxant and it helps to relax the uterus to keep contractions at bay. The bad news is it relaxes every muscle, leaving a very heavy and flushed feeling; I was barely able to walk to the bathroom. Your lungs can fill up with fluid so frequently you have to blow into a spirometer to help keep them clear and to measure your lung function. Basically, I felt like total crap. I didn't even want to read a book, do bed exercises or talk on the phone. All I could do was lay there and watch TV. One of the nurses told me that sometimes they refer to women on "mag sulfate" as "Mag Hags"—only when they're really bitchy about it. She probably wasn't supposed to tell me that but I thought it was kind of funny.

So this is what Willow meant by jail, I thought. How did she know? I know I was on and off mag sulfate more than anyone at the hospital. Because as soon as my contractions would stabilize to more like Braxton Hicks contractions, I would ask to be taken off of it. My regular doctor was out of town on a family emergency so I had a different doctor every day. But, sure enough, within 24 to 48 hours of going off the mag, I'd need to be put back on it because active labor would resume.

Dan showed up the next morning with clothes and treats. He also brought a beautiful sarong we had bought for our bedroom. It had a dragon on it because 2012 was the Chinese Year of the Dragon. The Chinese believe it's a very auspicious year in which to be born and many families plan to have children in that year. Dan hung it up on my room curtain and all the nurses admired it.

Because I was so bloated with amniotic fluid, checking Quincy with the fetal heart monitor was very difficult. It was like she was swimming laps in my uterus and it could take up to 20 minutes for the nurse to pinpoint her location and strap the monitor to me. Then I'd have to stay in some contorted position for about an hour sometimes so that we wouldn't lose the heartbeat. This happened frequently throughout the day and night.

The nurses gave me a steroid shot to help develop Quincy's lungs in case she was born prematurely before the magic 33-week point. The steroid shot put my arthritis into temporary remission, which was a great blessing. If I had to deal with the difficulty of moving from the RA and the mag sulfate, I would never have made it to the bathroom. It gave me one less obstacle.

For once in our lives together, though, we didn't have to worry about money. That felt like divine intervention. Dan had quit his job at Bridgestone Firestone as a store manager in November in order to work for himself doing tire export. It was going great. Before it took off, though, our income was very low and I was able to qualify for straight pregnancy Medi-Cal. It covered all expenses at the hospital. I was concerned that since our income dramatically rose and now that I was pregnant, which is considered a pre-existing condition, that I wouldn't have coverage. Fortunately, once you're on Medi-Cal and pregnant, you can't be removed and it covers you and your baby for a month or so after birth, too. It was so nice not to have to stew over finances while going through all of this.

When I found out I had to be on bed rest, my initial concern was how Dan could manage going to work and handling the girls by himself. We were lucky that our friends in Julian pitched in. They were great. Miss Linda would watch the girls some days after school, and Lydia would take Tabitha home after school with her so that Dan could come visit me at the hospital. Eva, our teenage sitter, and her family took care of the girls several times, too. Other friends made food and brought it over. Dan and the girls were well taken care of, which was a huge relief for me.

But I missed them all so much. Dan brought the girls to visit me a few days each week and Dan came most days. But I felt isolated from them and that one of my fears was happening already: time and attention away from my other children and Dan to care for Quincy. Was this the way my life was going to be from now on?

Even though I had some visitors and Dan was there for a few hours most days, I felt so lonely and depressed. There was a tiny window to the outside world in my room and all I could see was sunshine and another concrete building. I felt like the whole world was going on outside and I was stuck for God only knew how long. A counselor came to visit us.

"It's a difficult time, I understand. And we need to explain to the girls that mommy is not sick just because she's in the hospital. It's for Quincy."

But it plays with your head being stuck in a hospital bed day in, day out. You certainly don't feel healthy being pumped full of mag sulfate all day. I started to think about old age and all the reasons one could be stuck in a hospital. But I tried to stop that train of thought in its tracks because it was driving me mad.

One bright spot in the day was the nurses. They were all so nice and giving. Most of them worked part time at the hospital, taking care of their own families on other days. Some of them worked the night shift, would go home and sleep for a few hours, and get up to be with their kids. I told most of them about Quincy's situation. I asked all of them if they heard any miracle stories at the hospital. Most of them had stories. I don't know if I'd call them miracles, but they were definitely stories of hope.

One nurse a few years older than me homeschooled her four children, who she kept on a vegan diet, and worked part time at the hospital. I felt like a slacker by comparison. But she was incredibly nice and comforting. I could tell that she was not there for the money or to keep busy. She was there to evangelize and spread the word of God, of Christ. And she was there to listen and comfort. And she did. I told her about all the steps we had taken to try to effect a miracle for Quincy.

Right before she finished her shift, she asked me if it would be all right if she prayed for Quincy and our family with me. When I agreed, she placed her hands on my belly and prayed for a miracle for Quincy. I had never heard anyone pray so fervently before. At the end she asked me if I attended any particular church and she told me briefly about hers. It was evangelizing, for sure, which I usually find to be annoying and slightly offensive, but she did it in such a gentle and earnest way that, although she didn't change my mind about going to church, I didn't mind it.

A couple of perinatologists from Children's Hospital came in at different times to talk to me. It felt like getting visits from the Angel of Death. They were dry, humorless older men, men without spiritual beliefs you could tell. They would tell me what to expect with Quincy and they both advised that we just offer "comfort care." Dan and I disagreed with them—

Dan vehemently so. I was very confused about what I wanted. I didn't want her to suffer, but at the same time if there was something the medical team could do to save her, some surgery at birth, I wanted them to at least give it a try. They had no definitive proof yet that she was T18, because we eschewed the amnio. Without solid proof, the hospital had to do as we asked. There wouldn't be any proof of anything until a few days after her birth and the subsequent blood tests.

Day in, day out I continued to just lie in my hospital bed, uncomfortable as hell. The only movements I made were walks to the bathroom. When the doctors say you're on bed rest, they literally mean it—at least in a hospital. I could feel and see my belly getting larger every day, filling up with fluid. I could feel Quincy less and less as she floated somewhere deep inside the sac of fluid. Each day, I felt less like an independent human being and more like a human incubator. I couldn't see but I could hear some of the other mothers on the floor doing what I was doing, but most likely with healthier babies. I felt like we were all alien pods, stuck in a hospital incubating our babies.

But where could I go? I often fantasized about leaving. If I went home and put myself on bed rest, I would be at greater risk upon going into labor. Most likely it would come very quickly. And we lived so far from the hospital. I imagined about staying at a hotel or apartment next to the hospital. Even though we were doing better financially, we weren't doing well enough for me to do that, though.

I found it odd that no one asked me what I wanted to do. No one said, "Hey, Katie, do you want us to try to keep Quincy inside, no matter what the cost to you?" It was just assumed that since I was there they were going to do everything possible to "save" her, at least while she was inside my body. Upon birth, that would be a different story. There would be less effort to try to save her then. It made no sense to me. While she was in me, I felt like her life was more valuable than mine in the eyes of the hospital and doctors.

The reality was I was just in pain and discomfort. Wasn't that what motherhood was all about? Suffering for your children, if necessary? Weren't we supposed to want to die for them? But what if they were going to die anyway? Was I still supposed to gratefully endure this situation? I consider myself a loving and good mother but I'm not a martyr.

Dan could see what I was going through. I was in tears all the time, and that's very unusual for me.

"Why don't I call Self-Realization Fellowship and see if there's someone there who can counsel you?" he asked.

I hesitated at first but then acquiesced. When he phoned them, they set us up with a very kind nun from Germany. I spoke with her for about an hour on the phone and I found her to be very soothing and non-judgmental. I felt at peace, albeit temporarily, after our phone call. Also, I felt so thankful to have a husband who would care enough to think of this for me.

Dan brought me flowers the next day. When the flowers wilted it was the day before Valentine's Day and he brought the girls to visit. They showered me with handmade cards, chocolates, and more flowers. It was so good to see them. I missed them so much. I cried when they left. I couldn't wait to return home to our life. The three of them were on their way to the zoo for the first time. I so badly wanted to jump out of bed and join them or at least ask them to wait for me. But the day was so warm and sunny out and I knew Dan was looking for things to do with them. But it was pure torture staying in that room then.

A day later, Dan came and wheeled me in a wheel chair over to the cafeteria in the adjacent building. It was bustling with doctors, nurses and other hospital staff. It hurt just to sit in the wheelchair, I felt so bloated. We ate outside on the porch in the sun.

"It feels so good to be in the fresh air and sunshine," I said. And it did. But I also felt out of sync with the world and physically uncomfortable.

After lunch, Dan wheeled me outside to the garden and we had a long talk about spirituality and life. I can't remember exactly what we talked about but I remember crying and feeling so grateful to have this wonderful and wise man in my life. Even though I was stuck in the hospital, this was my favorite Valentine's Day ever. I felt so close to him.

After he left, the days dragged on. When I was off magnesium sulfate, I kept myself busy and positive with reading, writing emails, affirmations, and talking with friends. When I was on the mag, I just tried to relax and give into it, reassuringly asking myself when do I ever get the chance to just lie in bed all day and watch TV and have people feed and take care of me? It was a more positive way to look at it, rather than just feeling scared and sorry for myself.

One day when Dan and the kids visited, Tabitha asked me, "Mommy, do you love Quincy more or yourself more?" Kids have a way of cutting right to the point.

"That's a good question, Tabby. I don't know," I said honestly. "I suppose I love us both the same."

I felt exceedingly guilty because every day I had to fight myself from pressing the call button and asking for a doctor to come in so I could scream, "Get her out of me now!" Would it be so wrong to let nature take its course and stop the magnesium sulfate for good? I was told that if a baby wants to really come out, if it's really time, even the mag would not stop her.

As I grew larger, I'd beg the doctors each day to drain some fluid from my uterus. I'd say that it was unbearably uncomfortable, but somehow I was able to bear it.

"Can you still breathe?" one doctor asked.

"Yes—but not for much longer. I'm extremely uncomfortable."

"I'm not your doctor so I'm not comfortable doing that. It could start labor or possibly an infection or a placental abruption."

But the nurses told me a different story. They do it all the time and there are rarely any complications, several nurses told me. So why did the doctors want me to suffer so much? Did it really have to get to the point where I wouldn't be able to breathe before they would give me some relief?

I desperately counted the days for my doctor's return. I thought about lying and saying I couldn't breathe but I, too, was concerned about preterm labor, placental abruption and infection.

One afternoon Dan came to visit and our counselor took us for a trip down to the neonatal intensive care unit.

"It would be good for you to see this because this is where Quincy will be going right after birth. And if she needs further care or surgeries, there's a tunnel right through here to Children's Hospital," she said.

It was more disturbing than I had imagined. Some babies were screaming in pain. I had heard many babies cry before but I'd never heard sounds like these. And there were numerous babies here—some tiny, some looked pretty much fine and full size. Most of the beds were open with many tubes and computers attached to the babies. As I was wheeled through the neo-natal intensive care unit (NICU), I started crying. This was all becoming too much to handle. They say God never gives you more than you can handle but I was beginning to disagree. How much is too much? I'm generally a very positive person. I knew I would be handling this much better if there was a good chance for her survival. But with each successive ultrasound at the hospital, it didn't look good.

"But her heartbeat is strong. If her heart is so defective, how can this be?" I asked a doctor after one of the ultrasounds.

"It's your heartbeat that's making hers sound strong," the doctor told us.

The counselor we were assigned at the hospital was wonderful. She made a phone call and secured a space for us at the Ronald McDonald house next door. They were pretty booked up. This is a place where families with children in the NICU or at Children's Hospital can stay for a few dollars a night. It's like a hotel but with a common area for eating that has a commercial kitchen and plenty of refrigerator space. They provide some meals for you, or you can bring your own food in and store and prepare it there.

The days continued to drag on. As my belly visually expanded every day, I felt like I was going to explode. I asked a young female doctor who recently had her first baby a question.

"Is it possible that my water will just break on its own? I feel like I'm running out of room in there."

"Yes, it's very possible."

Chapter 24

Birthing Quincy

Sure enough, just hours after my conversation with the young doctor, as I was going to the bathroom to pee, I kept "peeing" even though the urge to go had stopped. The flow got stronger. Panicked, I pulled the call string on the wall. My nurse was just packing up her things to go home and she rushed back in and stayed with me for another hour or so. I knew Quincy must be very small because I was just about 33 weeks. And I was scared that she would come out of me and fall into the toilet, given the rapid flow of amniotic fluid.

"Let's get you back into bed and flat," said the kind nurse.

About five nurses came in to assist. I assumed that labor had to commence but they told me that you can stay pregnant for several more weeks after your water breaks, as long as you are being monitored closely for infection.

Oh great, I thought sarcastically. But at least I felt a huge relief of pressure from my belly. The nurses commented on how much fluid there was as it continued to gush onto my bed and the floor.

"You're going to be fine," a nice young nurse assured me.

Knowing how apprehensive Dan can get, I asked her to call him for me and ask him to come to the hospital. Even though they said I could be pregnant for weeks more, I knew Quincy was coming tonight.

After about a half hour, when the nurses noticed my contractions were coming frequently, they moved me to the Labor and Delivery room. The nurse there was stern and unfriendly, so unlike the amazing nurses I had grown accustomed to. She monitored Quincy's heartbeat like the other nurses had. Her heartbeat took a huge dive every time a contraction came. When the contraction ended, it picked up again but weaker. Most of the nurses looked uneasy but didn't say anything.

About an hour later Dan calmly walked in with his beautiful smile. I was surprised by his casual demeanor, though. I had expected Panic Dan. Apparently, he didn't think I was close to giving birth.

"She's coming today, I can feel it," I filled him in. "Her heartbeat keeps declining with every contraction. Like that time with Willow."

"Yeah, it's really scary!" the stern unfriendly nurse said. Wasn't she supposed to be comforting me? I know it was scary but it wasn't totally unexpected. The next question on the table was whether I was going to push her out or need a c-section.

The female doctor who had spoken to me earlier in the day came in.

"Wow," she said, "isn't that funny? We were just talking about your water breaking this morning." I knew it was probably my body responding to my mind's idea of a way out of my pain.

"We could have you birth vaginally, if you want, but I don't think it's a good idea because of the wide swings in her heartbeat. She might not survive the pressure of a vaginal birth."

"Okay, let's do the c-section," I relented. Normally I'm a person passionately into natural health, shunning medical interventions. But here in this hospital, feeling so very vulnerable and weak, I turned all my power over to the so-called experts. It was very humbling.

Right before they were about to prepare me for surgery in walked one of the Angels of Death—a perinatologist.

"So, as you know, Quincy's outcome doesn't look good. So what I'd recommend is no heroics—just comfort care," he said paternalistically, standing to the left of my bed as I lay flat on my back.

Dan, standing on the other side of my bed, became irate. "I don't care what you'd recommend. She's our baby. There's no proof of anything—only ultrasounds. You will take care of her and do everything in your power to save her!"

They argued over me almost as if I weren't there. I felt like they were going to come to blows. I could understand why Dan was being so emotional, but I didn't understand the disproportionate reaction of the perinatologist. He seemed to take it so personally that we were not going to follow his advice. As I started to have another contraction where Quincy's heart rate plummeted, the nurses shooed them out of the way and took me into the surgery room.

The whole procedure only took about a half hour. There was a large drape in front of me so I couldn't see what was going on. When Quincy was born, there was none of the usual fanfare or "congratulations." Only silence. They rushed her off to the NICU. I didn't say a word.

I went into the recovery room for a couple of hours. When they were finished with me, they wheeled me down on the bed to the NICU to see Quincy.

She was so tiny. Only 2 pounds, 9 ounces. She was attached to many tubes, and a ventilator. Well, I thought, our Sedona psychic was wrong about that. What struck me as so strange was her color. She was purplish black, covered in bruises from the c-section. I was feeling very weak but I leaned over and gently touched her little foot, telling her I loved her. She had the cutest little rocker-bottom feet, a trait of trisomy 18 babies.

Chapter 25
The Futile Fight

I went back to my room and rested. I pumped every couple of hours and had the nurses store the milk until I could feed her. She didn't need it yet as she was being fed by tubes.

"You're making a lot of milk," one nurse told me, "that's wonderful!"

"Not really," I said mournfully. "She can't drink it."

It was ironic that I had such a surplus of milk because with my other two girls I had a low milk supply. My 10 pound, 2 ounce Tabitha would have loved to have had all of this milk, I thought.

Dan kept me company for a few days, sleeping in the room with me. His parents as well as Miss Linda watched the girls in Julian. Whenever I had the energy I would have Dan wheel me down to the NICU with my tiny bottles of milk and some cotton swabs. I'd dip a swab in milk and put it in Quincy's mouth. She licked it up gratefully. I now had something I could do to comfort and bond with my baby. I looked forward to giving her these little milk treats. I pictured her getting stronger each day lapping up my bountiful, healing milk.

Dan took a video of her with his cell phone. He called her name, "Quincy, look at me," and she turned her head, opened her eyes and looked at him for a moment, then closed them. We marveled at her doing this. It was really amazing that she was so small, so premature but here fighting, listening, responding.

We put a stuffed animal in her bed that her grandma had brought over for her and the beaded necklace from the blessing way so she could feel all the love that surrounded her. I want to say that I sat by her bedside night and day but I just couldn't. I felt so awful from the surgery and the energy was so low in her room. I came down frequently to check on her but I didn't want to pick her up because she looked so fragile. And the doctors didn't want me to because she was attached to so many tubes.

The blood work came back a few days later. She had the same rare blood type as Dan: AB positive. Unfortunately, the blood work confirmed our fears: Quincy was indeed a trisomy 18 baby.

Quincy's nurses lied to us and told us she was doing well—so well that they were going to remove her breathing tube. We found out that the truth was that the Angel of Death, now having solid proof in the form of blood work that Quincy was trisomy 18, ordered the breathing tube to be removed so that Quincy would die. He did this without our consent.

Shortly after that Quincy took a downturn. Dan and I demanded that they replace the breathing tube, so the medical team complied. It was difficult reinserting the tube and they caused some damage to her in the process of reinserting it. She still continued to decline.

The perinatologist from the labor and delivery room entered at that point.

"What happened?" Dan asked him. "She was doing great so you removed the tube and now that it's back in she's not doing well. Why is that?"

"As you know, the blood work shows that baby is trisomy 18."

"Quincy," Dan said.

"Quincy. Well, as I've said all along we need to offer comfort care at this point. There's nothing more I can do."

"Nothing more you *can* do or *will* do?" Dan shouted next to Quincy. The doctor shouted back and they exchanged words once again. Later I felt terrible that we caused all of this craziness to happen in front of Quincy even though she appeared to be sleeping.

While I was extremely angry with the perinatologist for trying to take over and decide on his own to allow Quincy to die, and even pushing to expedite the process, I really didn't know what was best for her. Dan seemed certain that we needed to try to save her. Part of me desperately wanted to save her, too, but at the same time I knew she would have to have multiple surgeries just to have the hope of survival with no guarantee that the surgeries would even help her. Was this what she wanted us to do for her and what she was here to experience?

"We have to do something," Dan said to me. "We need someone on our side. Someone who will help her." He was in full fight mode.

I remembered presidential candidate Rick Santorum. I had read that he and his wife have a daughter, a toddler, who has trisomy 18.

Dan called Santorum's office and they gave him his wife's cell number. She talked to Dan for over an hour. They had a doctor in Philadelphia who helped them and she was sure he would help us. But how do we get Quincy from San Diego to there? There was just no way. And it was a Sunday. Perhaps we could call him on Monday and get the name of someone on the West Coast who could help us. Dan found her to be a very nice person. Even though we didn't agree with her and her husband's religious and political beliefs it was really nice to connect with someone on a human level who really understood what we were going through.

Dan also put an SOS on the Trisomy 18 Mommies Facebook page asking everyone for help. Two women in San Diego responded. They offered to come visit us at the hospital.

When one family arrived, my girls were visiting, too. We all crowded into the small hospital room. Their daughter was in a wheelchair. She was non-verbal and ate through a feeding tube. She was enrolled in a high school about a half hour from our town and had a special caregiver who took her to school and helped her mother at the house.

My girls really took to her. She tried to communicate with them through high-pitched squealing and grunts.

"Most doctors think that trisomy 18 babies can't survive. We're living proof that they can live and have lives," said her mother. I noticed that her older healthy son was sort of in the background. I wondered if he always took a backseat to his trisomy 18 sister. She had had 14 surgeries throughout her lifetime. The ultrasounds didn't show any problem. It wasn't until the girl was born with a gush of excess amniotic fluid that the medical team knew something was different.

This family left to get some lunch and said they would come back later that day with another family with an older trisomy 18 child. They would be there in solidarity and to be a presence for the doctors. Their purpose was to help break the medical community's misconceptions about all trisomy 18 babies dying or not being worth saving. To also help the doctors understand that trisomy 18 kids can and do live, Dan printed up several pictures of T18 kids from the Internet and taped them to the walls of Quincy's room in the NICU.

We had the uneasy and chaotic feeling of people who were running out of time. We made a few well-placed phone calls and pushed the hospital for a different perinatologist. They agreed to assign us a new one. The new doctor suggested that we have an ethics committee meeting with some of the staff later that afternoon. We agreed.

We brought the girls to the meeting because we didn't have anyone to watch them. They played quietly while the doctors and nurses explained the situation to us.

"Since we reintubated Quincy, it poked a hole in her abdomen and now her belly is filling up with air. It's difficult to explain but her esophagus doesn't reach her stomach."

"So what will happen?" I asked.

"Well, her belly will eventually fill up with too much air and explode," the doctor said.

"Can't she have a surgery to fix that?" Dan asked.

"She can, but there's no one who will do it. Doctors take an oath to do no harm and in this case they feel it would be harming her more than helping her because she's T18 and because she has all of these other health issues."

I kind of understood their reasoning. But as a parent, from an emotional standpoint, I felt completely helpless and angry. How could they not at least try to help her?

Dan couldn't see their side at all.

"So," I began angrily, "you're just going to allow her stomach to blow up and explode?"

"Yes," said the doctor somewhat sheepishly. I started to cry. I couldn't stand the idea of my little baby exploding. What an awful way to die, I imagined.

Since there was nothing more we could say or do, the meeting ended. Tahnee had just arrived and met us in the NICU. I was so happy to see her, happy to have someone else know Quincy for as long as she was with us. Tahnee and I went into Quincy's room just the two of us together and watched her quietly.

"She's beautiful," Tahnee said. "Have you done a reading for her yet?"

"No, I haven't. Seems like there hasn't been time."

"I'm not in a hurry."

"Okay." I held her little hand and shut my eyes, slowly going through the visualization process. When my mind had quieted, I saw three different images. First, I saw an old-fashioned telephone receiver with a coiled cord. Next, I saw a little fish swimming away from me, followed by a small butterfly taking off.

"Maybe the phone receiver is Quincy wanting me to call a doctor for her on Monday to help her. And the butterfly and fish represent her wanting her body to be all better so she can be free to take off." I was reaching.

When Tahnee had to leave to be with her family, I returned to my hospital room, completely deflated. Willow hung out with me and watched some TV while Tabby stayed with Dan downstairs in the NICU with Quincy. Then I got the call.

"Sweetie, it's Quincy. You've got to come downstairs. She's not going to make it. Her stomach ruptured," Dan said gently.

"Oh, no!" I wailed. I startled Willow causing her to cry, too. I grabbed Willow's hand and we rushed through the hall to the elevator, both of us sobbing in the hallway.

We saw the girl we met earlier in the day and her family in the lobby outside the NICU. She was there, as promised, with the other family. We exchanged brief "hellos," but I was too distracted and distraught to explain the situation inside the NICU.

We washed our hands and headed past the other NICU babies to the semi-private room where Quincy had been moved a few days earlier. I speculated that that's probably where the babies not expected to live are sent so that the families can grieve somewhat privately. I looked at all the babies and thought how pink and healthy they all appeared to be compared to Quincy. They're going to make it.

We all gathered in Quincy's room. I was so glad to find Quincy resting peacefully with no overt signs of a stomach rupture.

"Did you give her extra morphine?" I asked the nurse, hoping she could assure me that Quincy was feeling no pain.

"I gave her the appropriate dose," she replied defensively, not understanding the meaning behind my words. I was too exhausted to explain it to her.

Quincy had been unhooked from her tubes and dressed in a pink outfit with a bow on her head. Tabitha and Willow were crying quite a bit, especially Tabitha. Every 10 seconds she stood up and got a tissue, blew her nose and tossed it into the trash can.

"I can't believe Quincy Rose is dying!" she sobbed.

"I know, Sweetie," we tried to console them, but having no real comfort in our hearts for them or ourselves.

"Would you like us to take the girls into the other room? We have some bagels and crayons," one of the nurses offered. I thought about this for a moment, realizing it was a huge decision that was only theirs to make, seeing their sister for the last time. "I don't know… let's ask them. Girls, what do you want to do? Do you want to go color or… "

"Yes!" they said in unison, eager to leave the room of sadness.

Dan and I took turns holding Quincy for the first and last time. She was so peaceful. I could feel her heartbeat slowing down against my chest. We took note of her facial features up close, comparing them to the girls, to ourselves, as if she were going to live for 100 years.

I was holding her when her heartbeat slowed to a full stop.

"I think she's gone," I whispered to the new perinatologist. He took her from me and checked. He nodded in agreement. He looked very sad for us.

The staff was wonderful to us at this point. They took black and white photos of Quincy and packaged them for us to take home. We called the girls back in to hold their sister one last time. Their collective mood had changed; they were no longer crying. They each held their sister quietly for a moment and then they were done. We hugged some of the nurses, thanked them, and said our good-byes.

"You are a beautiful family," said the new perinatologist, clearly touched by something and definitely beyond the stoic, defensive demeanor he had exhibited earlier in the ethics meeting.

As we exited the NICU, I suddenly realized that in the chaos of it all we hadn't told our new friends who were waiting in the lobby about what exactly was going on with Quincy.

"How is she?" the girl's mother asked me.

"She's gone," I replied flatly.

"Gone?" she asked in shock.

"She's passed away."

Both of the mothers with trisomy 18 kids looked horrified. I could feel that they had stressed about this outcome for their kids every day of their lives. And here it was slapping them in the face again.

Chapter 26
The Incredible and Inexplicable

Only recently, about a year after her death, Dan and I realized how many days Quincy had lived. Quincy, meaning "the fifth," a "fifth-dimension being trying to inhabit a third-dimension body" lived five days. Not five times 24 hours but five calendar days nevertheless. And as I write this I realize she was our fifth baby together. Miscarriage baby, Tabitha, miscarriage baby, Willow, and then Quincy. And she was the fifth member of our family.

A few days before Quincy's passing, Dan had checked into the Ronald McDonald House next to the hospital with the girls. It was such a relief to have this available to us. As I said, we lived about an hour and 15 minutes from the hospital and the area was rather expensive. A hotel would have cost $200 and up per night. The Ronald McDonald house was about $10 a night. We checked me out of the hospital and headed next door to get some rest. I was deeply relieved to be out of the hospital, but still looking very much forward to sleeping in my own bed again. We were going to check out the next morning.

When I woke up the next day, I suddenly remembered that I had an appointment that morning to get the squamous cell carcinoma excised from my forehead. I had gotten permission from the hospital to be transported to the

University of California San Diego (UCSD) to have the procedure done as long as they took me right back to my room when finished.

Of course, I couldn't imagine keeping the appointment the morning after my baby passed away, while still raw and healing from a c-section. As Dan was getting the kids bathed and dressed, I sat on the edge of the bed and dialed the office number. I braced myself for Quincy to answer the phone.

Ok, I'm not going to cry, I'm not going to cry if she answers the phone, I told myself over and over. The phone rang.

"UCSD Medical Center, this is Angel, how may I help you?" the young woman asked.

I have never been more shocked about anything in my life.

"Angel?" I asked incredulously. "Your name is *Angel*?"

"Yes, how can I help you?" asked the kind girl.

"Do you know Quincy?" I asked, as if checking my facts to make sure there was a woman working there named Quincy.

"Yes!" she said enthusiastically, "She's my best friend."

I burst into tears, emotionally explaining the whole story to this stranger in about 60 seconds. If ever there was communication between our limited physical world and whatever spirit world exists out there, this had to be one.

Chapter 27

Healing

When we returned home it was a time of healing. Some friends had come over as per Dan's instructions and hid all of the baby stuff in our garage before we got home. It felt so good to be home but it felt different. It felt like I'd been away for six months. Things were in different places, some new stuff was purchased, some by Dan, some by other people. I made every effort to jump right back into our everyday lives. I went to story time two days later at the library. I was happy to see everyone there but selfishly hoping the girl who had been pregnant at the same time I was wouldn't be there. She wasn't. That night we took the kids to a circus. I had to stay active, for them and for me. If it was hard to push on, I just told myself that it was good to be back in life again and out of the hospital.

Between Tabitha and Willow, I think Tabitha felt the most connected to Quincy probably because of being the oldest child and because of her age.

"Mommy," she said to me one afternoon, "I think I'm just going to keep pretending Quincy is in your belly and talk to it."

"Oh, please, no, Tabitha," I pleaded, turning my head to the side so she couldn't see me cry. I couldn't explain more at this point.

I put cabbage leaves on my breasts under my bra to help dry up my milk. It was painful for a while but eventually the swelling receded. I had the desperate urge to call the hospital and offer my milk to any babies who needed it. I didn't, though, knowing that wouldn't be the mentally healthy thing to do.

Lydia made a special point of coming over every Friday for the kids to have a "play date." But I know she was just being a good friend and keeping tabs on me. She'd listen to my stories about Quincy, patiently letting me show her the photos.

After a few weeks I told her, "Lydia, I appreciate your visits but please don't feel you have to come over every week. I'm fine, really. I will be fine."

Some friends and acquaintances avoided us altogether, as if death were somehow contagious. Others would say hello, acting as if nothing had changed. Or they would ask the generic, "How are you?" At first I took some offense to this. Then I let it go, realizing that people's reactions, as all things in life, have everything to do with where they're coming from in their life paths and little to nothing to do with me.

We kept getting unusual gifts and packages from people. Some people felt the need to give our girls toys to comfort them, which was a nice gesture, I thought. One day I received a heavy box in the mail. I opened it and pulled out a large and very heavy teddy bear. It was addressed from the hospital. Inside the box was a note from a woman I didn't know. The gift was from a group of women somehow affiliated with the hospital, perhaps a support group of women who had lost their babies. They send these 10+ pound teddy bears to other women who have lost their babies to offer comfort and give them something to hold onto.

"Sometimes when we lose a baby, our arms will ache," said the note.

I know it was coming from a very heartfelt, generous, and loving place but I found the whole idea abhorrent. I put the bear up high on a shelf in the girls' room. Why would I want to hold anything like that? How sad would that be to wander around all day holding a heavy baby-weight teddy bear?

We purchased a beautiful baby urn with butterflies on it and had Quincy cremated. Prenatal Partners for Life generously made a donation to us that covered the cost of most of the cremation. We weren't sure where we wanted to put her to rest so we kept her on a shelf in our office for months. Every morning I'd kiss my fingertips and press it gently to the urn.

It made me sad to see it sitting there, bulging in the middle like my belly had. But I wasn't ready to lay her to rest yet. And we wanted to plan it well, and make it special.

My aunt, Mary Jo, who through email had encouraged so many people to pray for us, sent out this mass email to her friends:

"Thank you for having made this journey with us. I think the Lord has gifted Quincy with the ultimate healing and that 'where' she is now she will be forever beautiful, healthy, smart, strong and kind. And a miracle did happen… in our hearts. Gratefully, Jo"

I love that—a miracle in our hearts. It's probably true. Not the miracle I was hoping for but she did affect a lot of people in her short time with us.

I sent out emails to people who had prayed for us, letting them know that Quincy had died. It helped me somehow to heal, communicating via writing. The psychic we visited in Sedona wrote back:

"Thank you, Katie, for sharing with me about Quincy and her short time on Earth. My heart goes out to you and all your family as this was a major challenge for you all. I got your email the other morning before going to work at the Crystal Castle as the on-duty psychic. I found myself short of time so could not respond then. I was thinking about Quincy, you, and your family on the drive and as sometimes happens the Angels and Guides gave me a download about the situation. It's like hearing someone reading to you or showing you a movie in your inner mind. Thank goodness they also help with driving when this is going on.

"There were *big* clues in the coincidence of a Quincy and Angel answering the phone those days. No easy feat for those on the other side to arrange such clear messages.

"At any rate, they were showing me and telling me that Quincy is an Angelic Being that desired to bring a new frequency to Earth and in order to truly implant it she needed to be in the physical for those four days.

"She had been emitting the new frequency throughout your pregnancy and so you and all you came in contact with were receiving it for those many months. Thank you for having come to me for the session as I realize I too was blessed with this new wave length!!! I am truly honored, blessed, and deeply grateful.

"There are new ascension gateways opening and the frequency Quincy brought will assist many to find their way to the light.

"Being an Angelic Being it is very difficult to come into physical reality but part of what she desired to gift humanity. You all agreed on a soul level as well to be of help. Thank you, a tough job for the human self.

"There is nothing special you, your family, or anyone having been blessed with the new light need do other than acknowledge and remember that they carry a high frequency of Angelic Love Energy and it is to share it with humanity. You, or anyone else, do not need to be Saints in Body either, just strive to express the Angelic vibration as much as possible. The frequency is also implanted in mass consciousness and those who are able and in alignment will vibrate it as well.

"Allow yourselves the grieving that is normal but know that it was not all for nothing and that not all with Quincy's physical anomalies were also Angelic Beings. However, many were souls wanting to help develop compassion and forgiveness in others.

"In Grace and Light, Namaste"

She did not strike me as the kind of person to be particularly ebullient about anything so I found her email to be especially interesting. Specifically, the part where she thanked us for sharing Quincy's light with her. Could it be true that there are angelic beings that come here sometimes just to open up pathways of light, connecting two worlds together? It is an intriguing concept.

Chapter 28

Waiting for Mary Jo

Seven months passed and life moved on. The sadness lifted gradually but steadily. I thought a lot about the loss of what could have been versus what was with Quincy. My aunt Mary Jo arranged to come stay with us for a few days before she had to go to Rome for two years to do some translating work for her order. We hadn't seen her in about two years. The last time was during a period of transition, too, as we moved back to Julian and she helped us with the move. This time when she visited we were deciding whether or not to bid on our current property in Northern Maine. Other than our immediate family, Mary Jo was the closest to Quincy, even though she never had the chance to meet her. She listened for long stretches of time to my thoughts, feelings, and fears about Quincy. And she sent out all those wonderful prayer request emails. We wanted to wait until she arrived to finally lay Quincy's ashes to rest.

The house we were renting was right across the street from a very old graveyard, although it wasn't visible from the house until driving out of the driveway. A few days after Quincy's passing we picked out a spot for her in the graveyard. But whenever I thought of her being there, I couldn't bear it. Plus everyone has family plots there and I really couldn't even entertain the idea of any of us being there one day. It would also forever tie us to Julian, not something we were sure we wanted yet.

So Dan and I decided to scatter her ashes into the ocean near where we got married on Moonlight Beach. Also, I remember having one really great day at the beach with our family while I was pregnant with Quincy and after we had some questionable ultrasounds. We were in no hurry and just hung out enjoying the sunny day. Dan and I played Nerf football. I can't catch a football very well but I can throw a spiral really far. It was funny seeing the looks on people's faces as I wound up to throw the ball despite my giant belly. Of course, I didn't run to catch Dan's passes—just shuffled quickly. As we left the beach that day there was a group of people with some religious affiliation playing Tibetan singing bowls while watching the sun set. It was the best spot I could think of for Quincy.

Dan and I carefully ordered some urn jewelry in which to preserve some of her ashes. I bought a silver butterfly necklace because it reminded me of the reading I did for her where she was really trying to communicate to me that she was ready to be free and transform like a butterfly. Dan bought a masculine urn bracelet. He took care of transferring her ashes for me into the jewelry. The next day we packed ourselves up for the hour-and-a-half trek to the beach. I was feeling sullen that day, feeling that it was so unfair to have to do this, even though on most days I felt like I'd come to peace with her death.

The first stop we made was to a grocery store that sold latex balloons. We wanted to pick out five balloons, one for each of us. And five balloons would symbolize Quincy, "the fifth." Latex balloons when released soar high into the sky then pop into many spaghetti-like shreds and float to the ground and decompose. We wanted five extra large brightly-colored balloons. The staff was short-handed at the store that day.

"We'd like one of each of those colors with matching strings," I said. The lady behind the counter looked slightly annoyed with me for being so particular.

"Sorry to be so picky," I said, "but these are for a very important occasion so they have to be very special."

"All balloons are for special occasions," she snapped.

"Well, our baby died seven months ago and this is for a ceremonial release at the beach," I volleyed back.

She said nothing and finished the transaction, then turned to leave.

"Wait… do we pay you or do we pay up front?" I asked.

"No. They're on the house," she said as she continued walking without looking back.

Our next stop was Home Depot for a nice and affordable bouquet of pink roses. It was a Sunday and the regular flower shops in town were closed. We had picked out flowers from the same Home Depot years ago when we got married and our family scattered them around the ground by the Moonlight Beach overlook for a natural and free-form look.

My mood began to lift as we parked the truck and walked down to the beach. Even though I loved living in the mountains and country my favorite place in the world was still the beach. Any beach. When I close my eyes I can still feel the hot sand under my feet on the boardwalk as I'd run in my bathing suit and cocoa butter-slathered body down to the beach during my summer vacations in Ocean City, Maryland.

To our surprise, Sunday around sunset in September after Labor Day was quite busy at the beach. I am always one to avoid crowds and this situation was no different. We convinced the kids to go for a hike with us until we reached a relatively quiet spot on the beach.

I played some Tibetan singing bowl music on my smart phone, but due to a stiff breeze, it was barely audible. The five of us held hands and each of us said something about Quincy.

"Even though it was the hardest experience of my life, I'm so glad I got to know you, Quincy," I said and added, "and I'd do it all again." As I said the words, I wondered if I truly believed the last part about doing it all again. Sometimes when we declare something, it's as if we are hoping to turn it into reality through our words.

Dan and I each took a handful and threw her ashes into the ocean while the girls ran around. It was a windy day and the girls were stirred up by it. They were having a hard time focusing on what we were doing, or maybe it was just that they didn't want to.

Next we gave each of them a handful of flowers to toss into the sea after her ashes. The pink roses looked so beautiful in the late afternoon sea, floating gracefully on the tide as if dressing it up somehow, making the ocean even more special than it already is.

"Okay, everyone take a balloon," Dan ordered. This was the girls' favorite part. "On the count of three, let them go, okay? One, two, three!"

All five balloons ascended quickly into the sky. At first they made a formation that looked like the five on the side of a die. Then they merged into a single file line and headed northeast, to our future home. They stayed in this single line until drifting out of site above the clouds.

"Isn't that unusual? They all stayed together. And they weren't even tied," Dan said.

"Yes, it is," Mary Jo agreed.

I felt relief and elation. Quincy was free and so was I.

As we turned from the balloon release back to the roses adrift on the sea, we spotted an older woman gathering the roses from the ocean. Dan rushed up to stop her.

"Please leave them—these were for a memorial ceremony for our baby," he explained.

I had the feeling that she should have them, though, so I stopped him. It felt like she was going to give them to somebody or do something nice with them.

"It's okay, ma'am, you can have them," I said, still feeling free and light. I looked the woman over for a moment and got the feeling she was a nun for some reason. Like my aunt, she was not wearing a habit.

"Are you a sister?" I asked.

"Yes," she said in a German accent. "I'm a nun with Self-Realization Fellowship."

Of course she was. This was so perfect. I *knew* there would be some sign from Quincy today. She sounded exactly like the nun from SRF who had counseled me while I was on bed rest with Quincy in the hospital. I told her about Quincy briefly and asked if she had been the one to counsel me that day.

"No," she said with pity on her face. "I'm so sorry for your loss."

"No, it's okay. It was meant to be," I said, not feeling any self-pity, but still feeling free and happy. "It was months ago; now was just the right time to set her free because my aunt is visiting us," I said turning to introduce them. Having that woman show up at just that moment to collect Quincy's flowers felt like Quincy was saying, "Thank you for taking care of my mommy while she was in the hospital." Although we were only a few miles from SRF, what were the odds of an SRF nun with a German accent walking by at just that moment to gather our flowers?

Chapter 29

Big Changes and Unanswered Questions

Since the ceremony I've been thinking about what I've learned, how I've grown, and what questions remain for me. Maybe it's too soon to know. Maybe I'll never know. What is the meaning behind the number five as it relates to Quincy and our family (other than the fifth dimension, which I really do not understand)?

I tend to question the veracity of the Bible now more than ever. It obviously isn't a literal text by any means. In some ways, I feel much closer to the spirit world yet farther away from a loving creator, if that makes any sense. I know that in one sense God spared our family the enormous stress of taking care of a very disabled baby. But why did we have to go through all of that in the first place? I think we're a pretty great family and Dan and I are good parents. Why couldn't we have a third baby to love and raise like we wanted?

I tend to live more in the moment since Quincy. I take things more as they come rather than trying to control the outcome because now I realize that often times it's pointless. I hope for the best but I don't try to use the law of attraction in my favor even if that favor is for the greater good. I hold my wishes and desires loosely in the palm of my hand now rather than gripping them with an iron fist.

I'm still living in more fear than I want to. I have some post-traumatic stress. I cannot watch any news or read anything on the Internet that pertains to the medical field. I feel more stress than is good for me whenever I or anyone in my family come down with even a minor sickness. A lot of it relates to still dealing with a health problem of my own, I know. Once that's in remission, maybe I'll learn to let go and lighten up. Or maybe I need to lighten up and let go now for it to let go of me.

I see the mystical and magical in life more now. I look for it and find it. Maybe it comes from a desire to attach meaning to all things instead of just series of random occurrences. Maybe life is like that TV series *Touch*, with Keifer Sutherland. We could understand how all things are linked together if we just understood and followed the numbers. Dan says life is all about the law of similarities, like attracting like. And he adds that there's the pendulum effect. When the pendulum swings one way, it eventually has to swing back the other way if you hang in there long enough.

Dan and I have talked about whether or not all the work we did to try to help Quincy live made any difference in the length of her life. Dan tends to think so and I think it's possible. She was born prematurely, less than 3 pounds, with every health problem that a trisomy 18 baby could possibly have—and yet she lived five days. Most die in the womb.

Before Quincy, I was great at visualizing the future I wanted but, in doing so, I directed most of my energy there instead of being in the present and enjoying it. This is a huge gift from Quincy—the ability or awareness to live in the present.

I've been thinking a lot lately about where the soul of a baby in the womb resides. If the soul is reincarnated, does it really reside with the baby when it is just a few quickly dividing cells? Or is it somewhere else in another dimension? Is it with the mother, with the family on the outside until the child is birthed? When I was pregnant with Willow I had an odd swirling sensation in my cheeks. It felt like swirling energy centers focused under my cheekbones. I was especially aware of the movement whenever I did yoga. Was that her energy? Sometimes a new life in a woman's womb triggers significant changes that cannot be explained simply by the addition of a new life. It's as if the soul has brought with it issues to work out, and sometimes it's very positive and other times it's more challenging for the mother and family. But sometimes the change isn't unusual or noticeable at all.

A friend of mine had a son several years ago and later tried to have another child, but had a miscarriage. Instead of feeling devastated as many women would be, she was energized, transformed. I don't want to put words in her mouth but she told me that that spirit must have been a writer. Because before she was pregnant she didn't write much. But when she became pregnant and ever since, she hasn't stopped writing books, journals, anything. She feels that spirit gave her a gift.

I believe in choice. Sometimes it's the more difficult choice—such as continuing a pregnancy, especially one where the fetus has mental, emotional, physical, or developmental disabilities—that is the most rewarding one. You don't have to be pro life on the political spectrum to choose life. And sometimes life just chooses you. The day I was discussing the ultrasound with Dan and Quincy kicked like never before—and never afterwards—she was the one choosing life. I really think many women in my shoes at that moment would have seen it that way. Quincy was choosing life, however short it was going to be.

Chapter 30

Yes

I want to finish Quincy's story with an email exchange from my dear friend Rachel. Rachel and I went to court reporting school together in our 20s and have continued our friendship ever since. The funny thing is that court reporting is the least of what we have in common. Even though our life experiences differ significantly, it always seems like we are on the same spiritual life path. This exchange was written a couple of days after our blessing way ceremony:

Katie: Hi Rachel, I hope you made it back easily without traffic. It was so good seeing you guys. You both look healthy and great, by the way. Wasn't that blessing way cool?

Rachel: Yes, I can't tell you how inspired I felt as we drove away. It truly was amazing for so many reasons.

Katie: I can't believe how much love and time and attention to detail these women put into it. I know them from playgroup and play dates but we're all still relatively new friends—we've only been living here for about two years and I didn't know any of them the first time we lived here in '06-'07.

You know how we each have our great gift in life and sometimes others perceive it to be something different than what we perceive about ourselves? When I was listening to you speak yesterday, I was reminded for some reason about the time you spoke to me on the phone right before I decided to have an abortion. I can't remember the exact details of what you said but I remember where I was standing and how I felt from your words. My feeling is that your great gift and contribution to the world is that you know exactly the right thing to say at the right time. That's huge if you think about it. So many people are well meaning but say the wrong things, for some reason. Anyway, I just wanted to share that with you.

Rachel: Thank you. I consider this one of the greatest compliments, ever. Not to diminish the many wonderful things I have learned from you... of which there are many... I mean, even down to how much more thoughtfully and slowly I eat (well, sometimes:) after being inspired one day watching you... you have taught me much along the way. But I have to say, as of today, I consider your greatest contribution to be the very thing you are living right now. Unconditional love is the GREATEST thing one can aspire to touch upon in one's lifetime; not many are capable of living and loving without conditions. I'm telling you, I felt so completely inspired by your and Dan's commitment to Quincy. I thought about you as we drove home; I thought about you as I tucked Marin in. I was thinking about you when I woke this morning. So I did some writing and here's what I wrote:

An angel has come into this world asking to be loved. And my dear friend Katie did not stop to say, "I will love you for a lifetime if only you live long. I will love you for a lifetime granted you're everything I want. I will love you for a lifetime if the doctors deem you worth it."

No, it was my friend Katie who simply said, "Yes."

About the Title

I sat in the Psychic Portal one day before the book was finished. I had just about 15 minutes alone to myself in the house so I seized the opportunity to ask for guidance on coming up with a title. I closed my eyes and did my usual visualization exercises to get myself into a quiet and open state. The first image I saw was of a pregnant mother bear hugging her belly. I thought about it for a moment and figured that the word "embrace" might be what was being communicated to me. *Embracing Quincy*, I thought. Then I saw the rest of the words as just words, not images: "Our Journey Together."

Later, when I was still working on the book, I was worried that the title was too plain in that it didn't fully convey enough about what the book was about to someone who didn't know the background of the story. So I did some brainstorming on paper and didn't find anything better. Later that night Dan and I brainstormed together and we still came up with nothing (he already loved the title.)

Finally, I decided to check out thesaurus.com to perhaps find a synonym for "embrace." Guess what the first synonym was in the long list of synonyms for embrace? "Bear hug."

About the Author

Katie Marsh is an indie author and inventor. She also conducts clairvoyant readings for personal guidance. With health and fitness as lifelong passions, she spent time as an Ironman triathlete in the '90s and attended a vegetarian cooking school in 2000. Originally from the Washington, DC area, she worked many years as a freelance court reporter and as an official stenographer for the US House of Representatives. After that, she traveled the world for a year and a half, spending time in Thailand, Cambodia, Australia, and Hawaii. She now resides in Northern Maine with her best friend and husband, Dan, and their two beautiful daughters. They are working toward building an Earthship and sustainably farming their land.

Acknowledgments

Thank you to my little girls—all three of them—for choosing me to be their mommy. I don't know how it works but I do believe we chose to be together. Words can't describe the joy you all have brought and bring to my life.

Thank you to my dear friend Edmund Weisberg for his expert skill in editing this book. We've been close friends for 25 years and have had many adventures together.

Thank you to our friends in Julian for being open and supportive of our family and our choices and for helping us through a challenging time. And for creating a very special and memorable blessing way.

And thank you to all the amazing nurses at the Southern California hospital where Quincy was born. Your gentle compassion gives so much comfort to every one of your patients.

Thank you, Danny, for always encouraging me to follow my passions. And thank you for agreeing to share our personal family stories in this book. You are the love of my life and I cherish every day with you. I feel even closer to you and more in love with you now and every day we're together than the day we got married. You are my best friend and my destiny.

Further Reading and Other Resources

The following is a list of organizations that support families with children who have trisomy 18, trisomy 13, or other chromosomal disorders or families with children in the NICU. **Ten percent of the net profits of this book will be donated** to some or all of the following organizations:

Noah's Never Ending Rainbow
"The mission of **Noah's Never Ending Rainbow** is to educate, advocate, raise public awareness, promote strategic alliances and assist families who have children with trisomy and related chromosome disorders."
www.noahsneverendingrainbow.org

SOFT, Support Organization for Trisomy
"SOFT is a network of families and professionals dedicated to providing support and understanding to families involved in the issues and decisions surrounding the diagnosis and care in Trisomy 18, 13 and other related chromosomal disorders. Support can be provided during prenatal diagnosis, the child's life, and after the child's passing. SOFT is committed to respect a family's personal decision and to the notion of parent-professional relationships."
www.trisomy.org

Trisomy 18 Foundation

"Working together, we ensure families have the support they need and progress is made in the coming year! Your gift brings hope to families and their children coping with Trisomy 18 by investing in our efforts to fund research, build community, and shape dialogue in the medical and research communities."

www.trisomy18.org

Hope for Trisomy

"Hope for Trisomy 13 and 18 is a not-for-profit charitable organization based in Florida created in honor and memory of all surviving and Angel children with Trisomy 13 and 18 and Related Conditions/Rare Trisomies. The organization is now doing business as simply HOPE FOR TRISOMY to better represent its broader scope. The organization's Board of Directors is made up of families who have living and angel children with these conditions."

www.hopefortrisomy13and18.org

Prenatal Partners for Life

"Prenatal Partners for Life is a group of concerned parents (most of whom have or had a special needs child), medical professionals, legal professionals and clergy whose aim is to support, inform and encourage expectant or new parents.

"We offer support by connecting parents facing an adverse

diagnosis with other parents who have had the same diagnosis. We have many resources such as adoption agencies with clients waiting to adopt and love a special needs child should a parent feel they could not care for them.

"We believe each child is a special gift from God."
www.prenatalpartnersforlife.org

Miracle Babies

"Miracle Babies aims to become the nation's premier non-profit resource for neo-natal intensive care unit (NICU) patients and their families. Our mission is to provide financial assistance and support to families in need with newborns in the neonatal intensive care unit."
www.miraclebabies.org

The Most Important Section of This Book

Dear Families and Friends of Trisomy 18 and 13 Children, There is a wonderful organization called Support Organization for Trisomy (SOFT), which keeps a list of US hospitals that have performed cardiac surgeries on trisomy children. They update this list frequently so I was advised by their president, Barbara Vanherreweghe, that it would be best to include a link to that list in my book. The link is to a PDF file for the SOFT Table of Hospitals:

http://trisomy.org.s113588.gridserver.com/wp-content/uploads/2012/11/Cardiacsurgeries7-1-12WebSpecial.pdf

(If you have trouble opening this, go to http://trisomy.org, click on "Publications" at the top, then "SOFT Publications" and scroll down and click on "SOFT Surgery Registry." Then scroll almost to the bottom and click on Table of "Hospitals.")

Furthermore, they keep a list of names and phone numbers of families whose children have undergone various surgeries, the types of surgeries performed and what city they are located in. Due to privacy reasons, you need to email Ann Barnes at fbarnes@nc.rr.com and she will contact the families for you to see about arranging communication.

And here is a link to the page on the SOFT website that explains the SOFT Surgery Registry better than I just have:

http://trisomy.org.s113588.gridserver.com/professional/soft-surgery-registry/

Please keep in mind that hospitals' and doctors' policies change all the time. But if you are willing and able to travel a bit, you may find the help you need. Other families have. I wish you the very best of luck in seeking help for your child.

Please send me an email if you have success in finding a compassionate and qualified doctor. I'd love to hear from you! If you find one, and if it's okay with your practitioner, I will start a list of doctors on my website and add his or her name to it.

With Love,
Katie
www.embracingquincy.com

More Books
by
Katie Marsh

The Parenting Game Plan

Negotiate, Compromise and Explore the Parenting Journey Together

The Birth of Dying

Explore End-of-Life Issues with Your Terminally Ill or Elderly Loved One

by

Katie & Dan Marsh

Questions or Comments?

If this book touched you in any way, we'd love to hear from you. Please feel free to contact us via our website at www.embracingquincy.com. And if you feel moved to do so, please don't hesitate to write a short blurb about this book on amazon.com. It would be so helpful.

Thank you!

Katie

Made in the USA
Charleston, SC
17 August 2013